*Jim Masiello's Bare-Knuckle Approach
to Life, Business, and Politics*

$crew u

a memoir

JIM MASIELLO

with JASON LETTS

MINDSTIR MEDIA

SCREW U
Copyright © 2022 by Jim Masiello. All rights reserved.

No part of this book may be used or reproduced in any manner whatsoever without written permission, except in the case of brief quotations embodied in critical articles and reviews. For more information, e-mail all inquiries to info@mindstirmedia.com.

Published by Mindstir Media, LLC
45 Lafayette Rd | Suite 181| North Hampton, NH 03862 | USA
1.800.767.0531 | www.mindstirmedia.com

Printed in the United States of America
ISBN: 978-1-958729-39-7

Contents

Acknowledgments v
Foreword vii

1	Introduction	1
2	Growing Up Masiello	15
3	The IRS: Showdown with Uncle Sam	29
4	The Birth of SIAA	41
5	The Big Banks Come to New Hampshire	55
6	My Saga with Banks Continues!	69
7	Oceanside Pursuits	93
8	Stop the Bleeding	105
9	The Dairy Farm	111
10	Jim Masiello and the New Hampshire State Board of Education	125
11	Jim Masiello for New Hampshire	137
12	Screw You—And the Horse You Rode in On	153

About the Author 161

Acknowledgments

I'd like to extend my deep appreciation and gratitude to John Burk, CPA and Steve Burke, ESQ (fondly—Burk & Burke) for a combined seventy-seven years of sage business, personal, and estate advice in lieu of a Board of Directors or outside advisors. Also, my deepest thanks to friends and family and all those who have helped me through a unique career unselfishly and especially my soulmate and wife, Kathy, for all her years of dealing with a wide range of personal and business matters.

Foreword

There are people throughout American history, like Sam Walton, Henry Ford, and Steve Jobs, who's success stories inspire us all to do better and be better in our lives. There are stories such as Jim Masiello's that remind us that life is a journey—a marathon and not a race. Jim takes the bull by the horn the way a rodeo rider takes to the saddle. He never wavers in his desire to become more skilled and successful. *SCREW U* is an apropos title for this incredible book.

Jim comes from an Italian immigrant family, from very little financial means, and has a wildly confident attitude toward learning. Because of his tenacity and work ethic, he becomes someone to contend with in the business world. What fascinates me about Jim's book is his strength of character in his ability to see a new way of doing things when it comes to insurance companies. This is not a book filled with only successes but a book portraying the facts of becoming great, and in doing so, there are many mishaps, failures, and stumbles on the road to success. It's everything about the journey—good and bad—that makes a person's life, their work, and their passion meaningful.

So many of us believe that the status quo is the only choice in moving forward in a business venture, but not Jim. He took the insurance industry and turned it on its head. He did not become part of the big conglomerate but began an agency that worked to help the "little guy" with a small insurance alliance to become one of the big guys on campus. Before Jim Masiello and SIAA, an independent insurance alliance was fighting against the big insurance moguls. It was certainly nearly an impossible battle until Jim came along.

How a person becomes someone great is by defying *how things are done* and rewriting the playbook. *SCREW U* is the American dream. What happens when you come from financial *nothing* is determined by the courage you have to take and see a different path and then more importantly have the balls to take it. BRAVO, Jim Masiello.

chapter one

Introduction

Why should anybody listen to me?
Sometimes I still ask myself that. I'm the type of guy who doesn't back down from a fight and who stands up for what he believes in, but bragging has never come naturally to me. It doesn't matter what kind of accomplishments I've made over my long career in the insurance industry, the accolades I've received, or what impressive and important people have said about me, because I still think of myself as just a hard-working family man from New Hampshire who's been fortunate in life.

When I picture myself, who I see is the grandfather of seven beautiful grandkids I love; an interim coach of my son's sixth grade basketball team; someone who built a family foundation that supports education with scholarships for financially distraught kids; and, of course, my wonderful wife Kathy's lucky husband.

What I don't do is go around introducing myself like this:

"Hi, I'm Jim Masiello, the guy who stuck it to the banks and the IRS, getting away clean when I was in debt for over fourteen million dollars."

As much as that happened, and there's a huge can of worms that goes along with it, it's not that time in my life during the early '90s that entirely defines who I am. Those events seem like a lifetime ago, like things that could've happened to someone else and yet provide the foundation for what my life has become ever since. I try not to think about how easily I could've been wiped out and left completely destitute if the die had rolled just a little differently.

Even when it comes to my professional life, I much prefer to celebrate the relationships I have and the achievements of my associates rather than the top-line figures of how we built SIAA (Strategic Insurance Agency Alliance) from $0 into the $10 billion juggernaut it is today. Sure, it was nice to be recognized by Liberty Mutual and Travelers Insurance Company for being a billion dollar premium producer, but it meant even more when I'd meet with our member agencies while out on the road and they'd tell me about how joining SIAA had made a tremendous difference in their lives, how it was allowing them to put their kids through college, purchase new homes, and generally improve their standard of living. And that is why I refer to SIAA's role in their lives as being an enabler.

The work I put in developing the concept for SIAA has certainly made a tremendous difference in my life and that of thousands of insurance companies, independent insurance agencies, their employees, and their families. We revolutionized the national insurance distribution marketplace, but it's also allowed me and my family to enjoy a kind of lifestyle that most people could only dream about. It's a privilege to be able to spend time at our places in Florida, our condo in Boston, our beach house in Kittery Point, Maine, and a piece of my heart will always be in New Hampshire, particularly the city of Keene where I grew up, raised my children, started my businesses, and served two terms as the youngest mayor ever elected.

If it sounds lavish, it is, and that's where that old instinct to be reserved and modest comes in, because, truth be told, a life like this was not at all guaranteed for me. I grew up in a poor neighborhood in an area where people didn't have a lot and opportunities were not plentiful. My Italian family ran a neighborhood grocery store where I was expected to also work at a very young age. Even when we moved from my grandparents' home when I was eight, I always had a room to stay in. For holidays, my job was to help my grandmother make the family meals the night before, and that included everything from pasta to plucking feathers and preparing the chickens for my Italian grandmother from Palermo, Italy. I was very close with my grandfather, Matteo, who was from Naples. He had a pickup truck and would go into Boston to purchase imported Italian goods and products. He had established a map showing where the Italians settled in New Hampshire, Vermont, and central Massachusetts after clearing Ellis Island. He would then follow his routes to the many homes to sell his Italian friends the imports that they could afford. He worked three jobs and paid for his three brothers' entry into the USA.

What I picked up from all of that was a strong work ethic, something that not everybody got back then and seems to be in terribly short supply these days. My early experiences taught me that I had to rely on myself, but they also showed me that between my own ingenuity and exertion that I could have an impact.

As you might expect in an environment like that, especially back in the old days, I also came by a bit of a foul mouth and an instinct to hit back whenever I got hit, literally. I boxed in Golden Gloves when in college and played baseball and basketball for our high school. That was until my father told me that I could only play one sport—not that it mattered to him as he never attended any of my games or showed any interest.

Somehow, all of that—the willingness to fight back, the feeling of family that developed for those I worked with at SIAA, and yes, even the foul mouth—ended up playing an integral part in the giant pickle I found myself in later on when I was getting hounded every single day by multiple banks and the IRS over money I owed through no fault of my own.

For most people, this exact kind of situation is what would constitute their absolute worst nightmares, and I wouldn't wish what happened to me on anybody. Okay, maybe just a few people. But imagine yourself in a conference room of bankers and lawyers and, at other times, with IRS agents all breathing down your neck and trying to rip you apart over obscenely huge sums of money that you just suddenly found out you owed thanks to the Federal Government Resolution Trust Act that replaced all NH banks with out-of-state banks that really did not show much compassion.

How would you react? What would you do? What could you do?

At the time I had no idea what was going to happen. I risked losing everything I had except my core companies, comprising my insurance agency, real estate company, and travel office, which were owned by an irrevocable trust comprised of family members. The banks and IRS were banging on the door to my house. In some ways I'm still in disbelief about it and how it all turned out. I knew it looked bad when I heard the agents at the IRS had a special moniker for me.

They called me "the phoenix."

A phoenix, of course, is a mythological bird that, after death, rises from its own ashes to live again. The concept originated in Greek mythology and comes up frequently in popular culture through today, from Shakespeare's plays to J.K. Rowling's *Harry Potter* novels, for example. The idea of renewal that it represents is perennially popular.

But, as you might guess, when the Internal Revenue Service refers to someone as a phoenix, there's an entirely different meaning than the fantasy beast and hopeful connotation that we'd commonly have in mind.

To the IRS, a phoenix is someone with a massive debt load and yet a penchant for success that is likely to result in similarly substantial gross future earnings. This is the kind of person they can claw into, garnishing everything they're likely to make beyond a poverty-line cost-of-living minimum. What they were threatening to do was take everything I'd make for the rest of my life.

I would not meet with the IRS, so I gave my law firm and accounting firm each power of attorney. I remember getting repeated calls from my representatives stating that a regional manager of the IRS kept saying over and over that he wanted to meet me. I always had a thing about refusing to meet with IRS agents for any reason, which seemed like a sensible enough position. But the agent kept badgering and badgering until I finally caved in. Despite the staggering amount of money I owed the federal government, this agent from the IRS wasn't at all angry or harsh. In fact, the agent asked me directly, "Why haven't you filed for Chapter Seven bankruptcy given the amount of bank debt that you have?"

My response was that I will work out of the debt over time because the debt was the result of banks shutting down low-performing loans due to RTC pressure. The agent then added to the question, "Are you aware that if you did file Chapter Seven, half of your IRS debt would be forgiven? That was about $700,000. The agent then called me a phoenix! I started to put together why.

It dawned on me that they were looking at me like I was a cash cow, someone who'd be able to pay out for them far into the future. Plus, they knew my core businesses were protected from all outside financial concerns due to my prior trusts that held ownership. They knew I wasn't about to roll over and file Chapter 7, although the agent said that if I did, 50% of the IRS lien would disappear. But they thought they'd be able to milk me for everything I was worth far into the future, all over debts that had suddenly materialized because of the bank's incompetence and RTC actions.

There were some hard nights where I imagined being on something akin to a hamster wheel for decades in the future, spinning around and getting nowhere no matter how hard I worked. It was a sobering thing to contemplate, a stressful time of my life, and the outlook was truly bleak but nowhere as bleak as it would have been if my operating companies were not in an irrevocable trust.

Needless to say, it didn't work out the way the agent from the IRS expected—the way any of us expected—and I couldn't have imagined that this grueling episode would end the way it did. That's some clickbait, to use the parlance of the day. You'll have to keep reading to find out what happened.

In retrospect, banks could not get any of my core business assets, which were in irrevocable trust's company ownership and then the IRS lien. Still, it was a tough time in my life, with not just the IRS but also a number of big banks coming after me for millions of dollars each. The calls were incessant, the exchanges were often caustic and inflammatory, and there was more than one time when I had to draw the line and say enough is enough. I remember one time the week had barely started and the phone was ringing off the hook for the umpteenth time that day.

After gritting my teeth, I finally picked up the phone and let them have it.

"Does it seem like Thursday at two p.m. to you?" which was when we had a call scheduled. "No? Then screw you. Leave me the hell alone!" I said before slamming the receiver down.

Let's just say I didn't endear myself to my adversaries. A lot of people might prefer to suck up, flatter, or act obsequious in the hopes of catching some kind of break. But when you're in as deep as I was, I could see the writing on the wall that any kind of leniency was not going to happen. The only way was to fight my way out in the face of scorched-earth opposition—a veritable murderer's row of heavily financed organizations equipped with the best lawyers, all of whom were chomping at the bit to turn me inside out and take me for everything I was worth.

And I did fight like hell in a way that stunned them all.

Although the big events and twists in that story are certainly ones I remember, there was something far subtler that has stayed with me as well in the decades since, just a brief conversation really that like so many others could've easily been instantly written off and completely forgotten but has instead led directly to the words right in front of your eyes. I've always felt strongly that in the middle of any difficulty lies opportunity, and this might be the gem that comes out of that painful experience.

It was around this time when things were at their worst, but we were getting closer to the end, kind of a "darkest before the dawn" moment, when my lawyer said something to me that somehow got into my ear and has rattled around in my head ever since. And he wasn't just any dewy-eyed lawyer fresh out of law school; he was a top-level corporate lawyer who was flabbergasted by the bloodthirsty treatment I was receiving. At the same time, I could see from the occasional smirk that he appreciated my unfiltered defiance.

He said to me that I absolutely had to write a book about this, that no one would believe it otherwise, and my first reaction was to roll my eyes. *Yeah right*, I thought. Who would want to read about something more or less akin to a financial crucifixion? So I chuckled a little before indulging him in the thought.

"You think I should write a book about this? What would I call it?"

He didn't hesitate.

"Screw you."

Alright, he was right that I had said "screw you" often to the bank officers. I vividly remember the look of pompous indignation it inspired. "You can't talk to me like that!" the bank officer would wail.

"I just did. Do you want to hear it again?"

During the bank and IRS debacles, I was building the foundation for something that would revolutionize the insurance world. It started with the SAN Group, a regional network of local independent insurance agents in the northeast. The idea was to even the playing field by giving these small independent agents the ability to complete with larger agencies in their areas. Because of our network, they suddenly had the knowledge and competitive pricing necessary to grow their businesses. The SAN Group grew to sixty-seven member agencies and over $500,000 million in insurance premiums in northern New England.

This model evolved and stretched across the country in the form of SIAA, which provided a turnkey program that independent insurance agencies nationwide could use. Just like with the SAN Group, it turned small players into big hitters, giving them relationships and premiums they could leverage. Any agent could gain the maximum benefits that came with scaling, and as of 2021 SIAA was still the largest network of independent agencies in the United States. In so many words, this was my primary professional contribution to the world.

That conversation with the lawyer and the concept of recording everything I'd done in a book started to make more sense and become a real fixation for me.

It all created a great story, and I thought maybe this was something notable that needed to be down on paper. If I don't tell this story, it's something that would just get lost in the void of history, never recognized and never remembered. What if one of my grandkids wonders what we went through or how what we did impacted his or her life? I can't let this one fade and disappear.

It's been a long time coming, but now that I'm in my (semi) retirement it's time to take a crack at doing this tale justice. This is my opportunity to set the record straight, to put something together that's part of my legacy, and maybe I'll even take a bit of a victory lap after enduring years of the most excruciating scrutiny imaginable for a private citizen in our society. Hey, I deserve it, don't I?

But as much as the core of the book might be about this bare-knuckle brawl with banks and the tax-collecting arm of the federal government, and some people will be thrilled by a tale of how I managed to put one over on them all, I'd like to think I'm good for more than just one yarn. I've had a long career, and it's not a stretch to say that my accomplishments have had a faint impact touching the lives of every person in the country, albeit from the vantage point of the insurance market and the broad national range of institutions and customers that we serviced.

In all that time, there are quite a few other experiences I've had you might be interested in, stories worth sharing that can help you understand both who I am, where I come from with my approach, and what my background and perspective have done for me in the business world.

My role model was my mother! She managed our little store and endured my father's philandering. I watched her, day after day, making decisions that affected the store. She went through a double mastectomy and never complained. In addition, she was "Business Woman of the Year" and president of the Altar Society. She was an inspiration.

I've honed an approach to business leadership in my time working with CEOs and other top-level executives at some of the country's biggest and most prominent institutions. I've rubbed elbows with high-ranking political figures, some of whom would even qualify as personal friends and, as mentioned, I've spent some time involved with politics myself. I wouldn't be who I am if I didn't take the chance to share some of the views that my life and career have instilled in me, which you can take or leave.

But mostly my purpose here is to do what I've always done, and that's try to support my team, add value, and make a difference. Pretty much every nonfiction book has something of a didactic purpose, and if my experiences and the lessons I've learned can make a difference for you, this entire exercise will have been worthwhile. And I don't think it'll hurt if we try to make it entertaining but factual along the way.

When I think about my strengths or skills, a few things come to mind. Yes, I know a lot about the insurance industry and business in general, and I have experience with accounting that has served me well when it comes to preventing myself from being duped on one thing or another, but what I really bring to the table is an ability to see the forest for the trees, the ability to develop a vision that organizes things in a more efficient, more productive manner.

For a while I was Chairman of the New Hampshire State Board of Education as appointed by Governor Sununu and the Governor's Council. I took on the task of modernizing and digitizing the department, which at the time was still operating as though it were in the Stone Age, leading to all kinds of inconsistencies, miscommunications, and errors, not to mention just a general level of performance that was far below what it was capable of. My first action was to consolidate three independently located offices into one location, saving the State over $500,000 in needless annual rent. There's quite a comparison to be made between the work I did there and what I did within the insurance industry.

My point is that being able to process the rules for how things are done in a particular industry or circumstance and then imagine a way to reorganize them into something better is a skill that is startlingly hard to find. It's sure not taught at schools, and that's part of why I've always wanted to be so involved in supporting education. These kinds of high-level, critical-thinking skills are almost impossible to be automated by machines, or at least not yet.

Instead, the vast majority of people are just very comfortable going along with how things have always been, assuming it's the best when it probably isn't. Half the battle is helping people recognize that it's possible to devise new ways of doing things, then it's just a matter of rolling up your sleeves and charging ahead enthusiastically!

I am a firm believer that "change is good." When it comes to making change, it won't be surprising to say that relationships are key, and that's another area where I can offer a fair amount of advice. Now that I've left SIAA after thirty-eight years of founding and building a team of highly motivated staff members, it's the relationships that I miss the most, the people in my life who helped me and allowed me to help them. I think there's room enough in this book for some space dedicated to those who've been a big part of my journey, the people who believed in me, and the ones who took me up on my ideas. They deserve a great deal of recognition, because nobody can do anything on this scale alone.

So who is this book going to be for then? Who might reasonably expect to get something worthwhile out of it? Well, I'd say there are those who know me personally who might be interested in this kind of detailed account of what I've been through and what I think, but I'm hopeful this will be far more generally applicable than that.

There might be people who've been familiar with me over the course of my career, people who might recognize my name or even have a sense of my reputation in conjunction with SIAA over the years. I'm thinking of all those folks I met while out on the road, the ones who worked with us, wanted to work with us, or possibly were even competitors who recognized that I tried to do things the right way or had an impact in one way or another on the industry as a whole. There were so many stories I heard all across the country from people whose lives had changed because of us and their commitment to attain personal success, and this might be a special chance to gain insight into how that all happened and how it came about.

I would tell new members to our national organization that we were, in reality, an entrepreneurial-enabling business structure that would provide assistance, mentoring, and competitive insurance company markets to our member agencies and that they become instantly big by being part of a multi-billion national independent insurance agency alliance.

Then there are people who are interested in the insurance industry or want to learn more about independent insurance agent business owners. SIAA provided a turnkey program for how to market and run an agency as a business. Whoever you're working for, I want to lend you my expertise, because a smarter market and more knowledgeable participants help everyone from the person at the top of the C-suite all the way to the customer paying the premiums. Maybe there are even a few people out there who are thinking about ways to innovate in the industry and want to get a sense of how we got where we are.

But even beyond that, I'd like to think I have something to offer anyone who's interested in business entrepreneurship, leadership, executive performance, and what it's like leading a large organization, in this case a decentralized one with close to five thousand independent insurance member agencies. Your field could be completely different—you could be making computer chips, selling cars, or working in the hospitality industry—but many of the challenges you face are going to be the same as the ones I had to go through.

That being said, I don't pretend to have a monopoly on handing out advice for business leadership. There are no end of other books out there from people with different backgrounds and accomplishments ready to tell anyone who'll listen how they did it, but after everything I've come across, I really can't think of another instance where somebody did things the way I did them.

Maybe that's been the enduring benefit of being that scrappy kid on the block who'd never stay down. I didn't know when to quit, wasn't about to accept what other people thought was good for me, and I refused to shut up no matter who was around or how much leverage they thought they had over me. Those early experiences shaped me into who I'd become, and they gave me the confidence and sense of independence to do things my way, come hell or high water. And my way was to create a complete turnkey model for assimilation by larger regional insurance agencies and for their smaller and/or newer independent insurance agencies. The point was to allow all member agencies to focus on writing new premiums that would generate additional commissions and agency value—thus my focus. And my goal was to impress upon them that "big is better!"

I think that brings us back around to our opening question. Sure, I've been around the block a few times and have plenty of things to say, but why should anybody listen to me?

After all, I'm just a beachside grandpa who managed to escape fourteen million in debt while on the road to building a company worth tens of millions of dollars.

Hopefully at this point the answer is starting to come into focus for you, and it has nothing to do with who I am specifically. We were all colleagues and part of the team as working associates. We constantly reminded all relations that there is no "I" in the word team! I'm a data and performance-driven kind of marketing guy, and I'd take stock tips from a beggar by the side of the road if he knew what he was talking about. What matters is what the data tells us about the likelihood of a particular outcome implementing the concept of "size equals leverage" for the benefit of all.

Why should anybody listen to me? Why does anybody listen to anybody? Well, we listen to others when they have a track record of success, and that gives us a sense that it's going to be worthwhile.

I recommend hearing me out for the very simple reason that the things that I think and the ideas that I have tend to work out.

chapter two

Growing Up
Masiello

While I've always had to fight for things harder than one would expect or hope, and it always seemed like someone wanted to stand directly in my way, I tried to never lose the fighting spirit I grew up with. Let me show you where it came from.

What I hope you'll take away from these stories are some common themes to my approach that have worked out well for me over the years. I don't sit idly by while others do things; I try to be the one who steps up and does things. I'm constantly on the lookout for new ideas and techniques that can give me an advantage. I'm not afraid to take risks, and when they don't work out, I don't hesitate to use all options available to me when I need help.

I don't want to philosophize about the way I do things too much—this is not a branding exercise or promises for any magic formula for success—but what I do want to do is give you these stories as case studies in my experience in the hopes that they'll be food for thought and provide a sense of what's possible. If you're out there starting a business or beginning a new endeavor, you've got to be relentless.

It might be easy for someone to say, "Oh, this all happened in the '80s and '90s when there was no competition and it was possible to get away with stuff." Not really, and things aren't all that different now. The first step to taking advantage of the opportunities around you is to start believing they're there. I would stare at my plaque on my desk as I am now: "In the middle of every difficulty lies an opportunity!"

Early on for me as I was growing up, one wouldn't think I'd come by many opportunities in my life. One might think from some of the stories we've just gone through that I've always been a big shot with a huge amount of experience in financial matters from the beginning, but that couldn't be further from the truth.

As I mentioned in the introduction, I didn't have much that I was born with, but what I did have was a very supportive mother, grandparents, and mentors who believed in me. The turning point was in my junior year of high school. A priest who had befriended me asked my parents for a meeting with me and him. At that meeting, he said, "Your son has choices of which way to go in life—he can continue down the path he is on or apply himself, change his friends, and take school seriously." That was a wakeup call from a person I greatly admired.

I didn't have the traditional family structure that many enjoyed, as I was mostly influenced by my grandparents who passed through Ellis Island into the United States with no cell phones, food stamps, house allowances, etc.–essentially with only the clothes on their back and a small bag of their worldly possessions. They were Italian immigrants, my grandfather from just outside of Naples and my grandmother from Palermo. While many Italian immigrants stayed in New York City and the nearby vicinity, for reasons I'm not entirely sure of my grandparents moved farther into the northeast and landed in Keene, New Hampshire. This was a small, working-class city back then, and I had to learn fast that I was expected to make a contribution for the good of the family.

I remember when I was eight years old and my grandfather, with my grandmother's encouragement, bought a four-tenement house in a particularly poor part of our city. They built a small neighborhood store influenced by imported Italian products in the front on the ground level, allowing me to get to know many of the poorer families around us as I worked the store.

While the store was in the front, we lived in the back and rented out the two tenements on the second floor. As you might gather, there were a lot of people around in a tight area, surviving in conditions that would certainly be considered uncomfortable today. But with hard work and helping each other, we managed to make a living in a tough situation, made tougher by my philandering father having to steal money to support his other family.

Considering I was the first grandchild, there was always a strong expectation that I would pitch in whenever possible. Fortunately, being around the store and performing whatever jobs needed to be done was something I enjoyed, and there were times when I felt like I could've run the place entirely by myself if I had to.

The requirement that I help out was not limited to the store though. When my grandmother would prepare meals for family gatherings, I was right there in the kitchen with her, peeling and chopping. True to type, she was a legendary cook with a magic touch for food that seems impossible to replace now. Even when I wasn't living with my grandparents, there was always a room for me there, and I'd stay with them fairly often.

So, for eight years I worked in the store on weekends and even every weekday while I was in Catholic grammar school. All my friends were altar boys. I wanted to be one as well but for some reason was not allowed. According to the priest, I was a little too mischievous to qualify, but that didn't prevent me from involuntarily taking on an active role in the church while I was young. I would involuntarily go to the convent on Friday after school and help the sisters make the Eucharist for Sunday mass.

While I spent a lot of time living with my grandparents, my mother was a big part of my life to varying degrees at different times. I didn't have much of a relationship with my father, who was a known philanderer who resented that I was the reason he had to marry my mother. He fathered another son (never met as such), but my father and I had very little to do with one another, and we were never close. Despite not being very endeared to each other, he still managed to weigh on my life now as someone I did not want to grow up and be like.

When I got into high school, I played basketball and baseball when I wasn't doing homework or working in the store, but my athletic pursuits didn't really please my father, who was adamant that I could only play one sport in high school because it was interrupting the time that I need to spend working at the store. This was baloney and a position he seemed to take purely out of spite. I ended up choosing neither basketball nor baseball though, picking football my junior year of high school and then starting for the high school varsity football team.

It would've been nice if that was the only conflict I'd had growing up, but that was far from the only time someone tried to dictate what would happen in my life.

I was almost not allowed to graduate high school with my diploma because some person or student placed a cow in the auditorium where the graduation ceremony was to take place the next day. The principal summoned me to his office, and I went accompanied by my mother, whose reputation for having a fierce side was well known to the principal. The principal told me that if I admitted to being responsible for bringing the cow into the auditorium that he would give me my diploma.

Under my breath, I whispered, "Screw you," and that was much nicer than my mother was.

"You give him his diploma NOW!" she hollered, channeling wrath onto him, the likes of which he'd never before seen. "Don't stand there accusing him of things you don't know anything about!"

When my mother finished, the principal was successfully cowed. He said he'd give me the diploma, but he knew that I was the one responsible. Around that time, pictures of the cow in the auditorium surrounded by its waste and the story of it being there right before graduation were well-circulated, going viral as much as things could back in the '70s.

I'd encountered that principal a number of times in passing after graduating from high school but finally had the occasion to have a real conversation with him a number of years later when I came by to watch a high school football game and he happened to be there. Being there together in the stands while watching the high school team playing on the field below, I could vividly recall playing on the same team on the same field, but the years had slipped by seemingly in an instant.

"Sid, I know what you're thinking, so I might as well get this discussion over with. Yes, I am the one who was responsible for putting that cow in the auditorium," I admitted.

It might be worth mentioning that by this time I was thirty-two years old and mayor of the city.

"I knew it," he said, looking at me and breaking into a laugh that we shared. It was nice to finally have some closure on that and get to a place where some of those things from my youth were just water under the bridge.

But back to when I was a young kid fresh out of high school. I still had my duties at the store, but I also got a job at a shoe factory for two summers. My hours were from 7 a.m. to 4 p.m., and I handed the checks and other meager money I received to my mother to save for me. After saving diligently for two years, I was able to attend business school for the first year, but when the second came around I was flat broke and unable to continue.

For a lot of people, especially the ones who came from places like I did, an unplanned hiatus like this because of financial challenges would've spelled the end of college dreams and higher ambitions. I could've ended up just working in the family store for the rest of my life, struggling to get by at a subsistence level, and there were moments when it seemed like I would have to do that.

I did have to go back to work, this time delivering table talk pies six days a week, but I kept saving and eventually managed to scrape together enough for that second year of business school. And while I was attending school, it wasn't like I was able to sit back and coast, picking up a book now and then as you see some college students do. No, I continued working straight through school. Every Friday afternoon I would thumb from Boston the eighty-five miles back to Keene so I could spend part of the weekend working in the store, and driving taxi until 2 a.m. Sunday. Late Sunday afternoon I'd then take the same trip back to Boston.

During the week when I wasn't in class, I spent time working in the college cafeteria cleaning the floor, picking up messes, and doing the washing. It was the absolute definition of a crappy job, but it did allow me to eat for free, and being able to keep my expenses low was a boon when it came to having enough to squeak through the program.

There were times though when it was particularly trying to have to work this hard to get by. One time, another student got into the habit of deliberately dropping things on the floor and then telling me to pick them up and laughing with his asshole friends. This game didn't last very long, and as soon as it became obvious that he was making a mess on purpose, he got a much different response.

"Screw you," I told him, and he jumped right up out of his seat and came at me.

That was a mistake on his part, because he ended up right on the floor in the mess he'd made and needed somebody's help picking him up. I sure wasn't about to do it.

Things got easier after that, and no one else tried any shenanigans, but it was still an around-the-clock effort to get my life to function with the expenses I had. I even managed to spend some of what little free time I did have boxing in the Golden Gloves, and I was able to play on the basketball team, even becoming the captain.

My studies weren't the easiest either, and I applied myself as hard as I could to get the most out of them. Considering what I had to do for every dollar that these classes cost, I was sure going to extract the maximum value from them. That doesn't mean I got an A on every test, but I learned a lot and took my studies seriously in a way many other students didn't.

I'll even go as far to say that many other college students I was around couldn't have done what I did to make it through school. If it wasn't for the demands I had growing up, I wouldn't have known what I was capable of and simply given it up. But as it was, I believed in myself and what I could accomplish, and I stuck with the jobs, no matter how bad they were, and the classes that came one after another and carried high expectations.

Looking back on it all, these were the formative years of my life, and if I hadn't had them and gone through them this way, I wouldn't have been able to handle what came later and become as successful as I did. I can certainly imagine how nice it would've been if things had been easier or if I had more, but right now from where I'm sitting, I wouldn't change anything. My belief is that hard work produces luck and success.

After graduation, my education in the field of hard work and scraping by continued. The first job I got was with Pittsburgh Plate Glass (PPG) in the Management Program, and while performing that job in Springfield, Mass, I had a room at the YMCA. I found though that this wasn't the career for me. Being a management trainee for a large national company was a decent job, but I couldn't get over the manager, who I didn't have a shred of respect for. I still remember the guy, Mr. McDonald.

He'd arrive at the office every day around 9 am, park his shiny Cadillac, don a straw hat like he was Old McDonald working on the farm, and then go into his office. That's it. He'd just hide out there until the day was over, having spent the entire day without interacting with any of us or contributing anything. I had developed a strong appreciation for hard work and couldn't stand his freeloading, and I knew instinctively that

I just didn't want to be like him. Working hard at my job so that I could one day move up into his position and sit around all day wasn't what I had in mind for myself.

So one day I went to his office with the intention of quitting my job. When I reached the door, his secretary said he was too busy to see me.

"But I can see him reading a newspaper right through the window. I'm going in there!" I said.

The secretary put up a little bit of a fight but eventually caved. No doubt she knew I was right and couldn't argue it all that much. When I opened the door and stepped into the manager's office, he had a subtle look of shock that someone else could be occupying the room with him.

"Mr. McDonald, you don't know me, but I'm terminating my management training position. Honestly, I just don't ever want to go through life like you," I said.

He smiled at my comment, clearly relishing the reference to his comfortable lifestyle.

"You're making a big mistake and will regret this," he said. If that was his attempt to change my mind, it definitely didn't work.

"Thank you," I said before turning to the exit, seeing that he'd proven my point yet again. He didn't really care about me, the work we were doing, or the company we worked for, and I was having none of that.

That left me walking out of the only job I had with the ominous words that I'd regret it looming over me. I was six weeks away from getting married and having more responsibilities than ever. There was no way he could be right, right?

At this point, I did what came naturally to me, and I went out and got back to work, but things were going to be a little bit different from now on, and that job at Pittsburgh Plate Glass would be a big transition into working for myself, which I found to be vastly superior.

What I did was start selling life insurance on a commission-only basis. I went all over. I busted my tail, and I struggled with it. In my first year I made a whopping $2,300. There were times when I wondered if the insurance market was a bust and impossible to earn a decent living from. If only I'd known where it would lead me…but that experience did help inform my perspective when I created SIAA, formulating it so that the independent insurance agents doing the same job I did would have the enabling support and education necessary.

But since the money was so modest then, I did have to do some other work to get by. On weekends I would handle open house showings for a developer, which also gave me a little taste of the real estate industry. Every time somebody bought one of the houses I showed, I received the princely sum of exactly fifty dollars. But things were looking up, and my second year of selling insurance resulted in skyrocketing growth all the way to $5,100. That was starting to look more like decent money someone could live on.

While we were starting to find our financial footings as a family and I was still enjoying being relatively newly married, I knew that I was still in a tenuous position and could not at all afford to coast by. This meant applying myself again to this new field that I had some experience in but was still exploring. I took courses and focused on learning the life insurance business, and of particular benefit to me were colleagues and a supportive atmosphere in my office that helped me get up to speed quickly.

Between the educational course and the knowledge that I absorbed from my peers, my earnings jumped to a staggering $13,000 that year. OK, so I lied about my age (twenty-three), but did have a minimum age of twenty-five for the position and was promoted by Occidental Life insurance co. I was rich! This also coincided with some of the first substantial financial deals I made, this one involving an elderly schoolteacher who inherited the home we were renting.

Don't worry. I didn't have to say "screw you" to her at any point. But we did work out a way for me to purchase the home, and she was the one to present some generous terms that made a big difference to a young family. I think she had a sweet spot for us.

Her offer was for us to give her one hundred dollars a month for six months, and in exchange she'd reduce the price of the house by another $600. This would become our down payment on a government FHA program mortgage, which only needed 3% upfront in order to make a purchase.

Things were moving in the right direction for us. We were putting down roots and getting established, but protecting our source of revenue and building on what I'd started in the insurance industry was still the priority. I'd already gone from $2,300 to $13,000. What was stopping it from becoming $25,000 or $100,000? My talent and knowledge in the field were the only things holding me back.

At twenty-three years old, I became immersed in the life insurance business, and I learned there was more to the business than just policy terms, marketing, and the mechanics of running an insurance business. Over and over again I was struck by how much networking and relationships mattered. There was a degree to which the warm feelings we had around our office extended to every office in the insurance business, and I got to work getting to know people and building friendships just because I never knew when they would come in handy.

The impact I was able to have at a very young age as a professional was striking. I served as president of our local life insurance association and was then elected president of the New Hampshire life Underwriters Association, which had over six hundred members, at age twenty-six. In some ways it seemed like the transition from broke graduate struggling to get by to a prominent statewide figure in the field of insurance happened in the blink of an eye. But really that's just because I worked so hard that it all went by in a blur.

One of the things I did during that early period, at age twenty-five I believe, was to dip my toe into the ownership side of the business. I borrowed $17,000 on my successful life insurance commissions and became a 50% owner of a small independent insurance agency. Part of what made this easy was that the current owner, like that marina owner, did not have his heart in the business and was looking to start making an exit. The agency owner was known to be a bookie in another New Hampshire city, and I suppose that was what he wanted more time to be able to do.

Regardless of his personal pursuits, he was a very nice person who did right by his business even as he was directing himself farther and farther away. In this case he did personally handle the financing between my new partner and me, and the relationships we all built together continued to pay dividends.

Even though I was young—younger than many of the other guys I worked with—what set me apart was my strong drive and hunger to make this work. I aggressively went after sales, maximizing everything I could. To me this all just felt like a natural extension of my work ethic and desire to fulfill my obligations to my family, but I quickly learned that not everyone was going to be so friendly and supportive.

After the purchase, the VP of one of our largest insurance partners summoned me to his office. He didn't mince words or waste time with pleasantries.

"Who in the hell told you that you could buy that agency?" the guy said straight off.

I shouldn't have had to say this, but I reminded him that we were independent agents who didn't need each other's permission to do things, and his expression only curdled further.

This VP told me that his company was pulling out of our agency, which was going to be a painful loss, no doubt about it. We needed those sales, but there was only going to be one alternative without them, and that was to get out there and work even harder.

Some meetings are about talking and coming to an agreement, and others are just confrontational, and I could see that this was going to be among the latter. There was no point talking to him or trying to reason anything, since he'd only been condescending and had already made up his mind. He saw me as just a kid and clearly didn't have any respect for me. After his company promise to leave, I had a good response for him. This was no elderly schoolteacher.

"Screw you," I said, and I left him with his mouth open. No one ever spoke to him like that, but I wasn't going to take his smarmy condescension lying down.

Despite setbacks like those, I continued to work hard and do right by the people around me, and fortunately the positives far outweighed the negatives, and I was able to build a good reputation.

Also at age twenty-seven, I was elected to the city council and appointed chairman to the finance and public works, something that was impressive back then but is truly a rare feat for someone today. For those keeping track, I was serving on the city council, running a growing insurance agency, and tending to me family. Overall, I was very busy, just as I was in college and before that growing up.

Somehow, I was able to handle it all though, and the result was that I was elected mayor of Keene, New Hampshire at age thirty-one, becoming the youngest mayor in the history of the city. Six prior mayors had publicly endorsed my opponent the weekend before the election, but by then my supporters and my hustling had already taken its toll on the race, which was all but over.

The city's old guard did everything they could to stand in my way, not because they disagreed with my ideas. They said I came from the wrong side of the tracks, and that someone from my neighborhood shouldn't be mayor. There were plenty of opportunities to say "screw you" then. While they were right about where I came from, it only served to make me more determined to prove them wrong about how I couldn't be mayor.

The night of the election found me trailing by quite a few votes to my opponent. We had five city voting districts. My home district had not finished the vote counting until 2 a.m. When my home district voted strongly for me, we won by a narrow margin. Two years later I won re-election with 70% of the city-wide vote and announced then that I would not be running again.

Stepping into that office and sitting behind the desk for the first time while those old guys bristled and grumbled far away from city hall was a sweet moment, for sure. Now I just had a job to do. And how did it work out? Well, I was reelected to a second term with over 70% of the vote. Serving my city was something I'll always be proud of, but it was really only the beginning of my story.

From there, I became president of the chamber of commerce and the regional YMCA. The state legislature appointed me to the New Hampshire Insurance Advisory board. I was also appointed to the NH Municipal Association Executive Board. And the governor appointed me chair to the fuel crises statewide committee.

And while all this was going on, I was still working and growing my insurance agency, which had adopted and implemented a "cross-selling" strategy that created profit centers in real estate, commercial leasing, residential development, construction, and travel.

Everything was going in the right direction and growing larger, including my family, which was always my first priority. My kids were getting bigger, and I enjoyed talking to their teachers and taking them to their sports teams. My daughter in particular had swim team practices at 6:30 a.m. The kids would even come to mayoral functions with me and met President and First Lady Ford when we hosted them at our home several times.

Later on, Bush 41 and Barbara stayed with us and would make breakfast for the kids before school. Prior to this, then-President Gerald Ford and Mrs. Ford stayed with us twice.

All this for a kid who started out in a tenement behind a family-owned corner grocery store, and I'd made it all the way to having the president of the United States be a guest in our home and we in the White house for a presidential dinner for the German president.

chapter three

The IRS: Showdown with Uncle Sam

Like most people, I don't have a particular fondness for paying taxes. Even though I understand the purpose it serves, it's just not my or anyone else's favorite thing to do. In fact, my personal approach is to be as hands off about the whole thing as possible. My accountant tells me how much I need to pay, I hold my nose, write a check, and give it to my CPA to pop in the mail. The goal is to think about it as little as possible. As a matter of fact, I only sign my tax return, and I have not reviewed a tax return in over fifteen years.

Even when IRS audits became a routine thing for me, I tried to keep the entire process at a distance so that I could keep focused on the work that I had to do.

But there was one time in my life when I had to think about bank debt and taxes and the IRS quite a lot, and it ended up being one of the most difficult periods of my life, along with my battle with the banks, which will come next. This was back in the late '80s and early '90s. It was much earlier in my career, predating my immersion in SIAA, making it really a crucial juncture in my journey.

When I had so much going for me with an idea and a direction I knew would take off, this was the exact wrong time to get caught in a quagmire with the IRS, and this one threatened to pull me under.

As noted, this was the mid '80s under the Ronald Reagan administration, which is generally known as a period of tax cuts and federal deregulation coming after the stagflation of the Jimmy Carter years. Reagan's famous line was that this was "morning in America," marking the era as a time to get to work and unleash our productivity now that regulatory and taxation impediments had been cleared out of the way. Considering Reagan was reelected in 1984 with 58.8% of the vote, winning every single state but Minnesota in an unprecedented landslide, that was a popular message and one that I was on board with.

But it didn't come without some unintended or perhaps just unfortunate consequences, at least for me.

After the election, Reagan signed the Tax Reform Act of 1986 into law, which as the name states overhauled the tax code and continued the adjustments that had been made in the earlier Economic Recovery Tax Act of 1981. The Tax Reform Act of 1986 most notably reduced the top tax rate from 50% to 28% while raising the bottom tax rate from 11% to 15%. Never before had the top rate been lowered and the bottom rate raised at the same time. While I was in the upper echelons, there were some other implications of the law that received much less attention but nonetheless had a profound impact.

A lot of people were caught off guard by aspects of the law or simply hadn't been informed enough about what it contained. An ABC News poll at the time found that 63% of Americans were so in the dark about it that they couldn't even say whether they felt it was good or bad.

Although I certainly consider myself an informed person, there were significant aspects of this complicated and dense bill that I hadn't fully been aware of until after it had passed. Perhaps part of how they justified the big cuts to the tax rate was that they made the change that capital gains would be taxed as ordinary income, something that would be reversed later. They also tightened the rules governing depreciation, so that those assets needed to be accounted for and paid all at once, and the rules for how deductions were handled.

Those were the provisions that ended up having an outsize impact on me. I was a person of means with a variety of assets and interests, substantial income, complex banking relationships, and accounting methods predicated on the rules of the day. When those rules changed, suddenly it was like the ground had given way beneath me.

I still remember that day when I got that first letter informing me that there was a suspected tax shortfall and that tax fillings impacted by the 1986 tax code changes were being audited. It was one of those pieces of mail you knew you didn't want to open, because it was going to change your life, and not in a good way. When I handed the packet over to my CPA, the grim mood was palpable. We had to scramble to come up with absolutely everything we had so that it could be handed over. While we were organized and responded swiftly, the requirements and the effort needed to meet them was onerous and grueling. The process quickly weighed on me, and that was even before we found out what the final toll came to.

When it turned out that I owed $1.4 million to the IRS as a result of these changes to the tax law, it would be an understatement to say that I was shocked. First of all, I'd never owed a dollar to the IRS in my life. Never filed late. Never taken any liberties or what have you. Everything was by the book, except we were dealing with a different book now, and I'd been caught up in the change to a degree I couldn't fathom.

Needless to say, I didn't have about a million and a half in cash, not even close. And we're talking about $1.4 million in the mid '80s. Adjusted for inflation, that would be equivalent to over $3.3 million today. Could you imagine opening up your mailbox today and getting a letter saying you owed that much money? What would you do? How would you feel?

I felt beside myself in disbelief that this was really happening to me. I've taken my share of accounting courses and understood how the system had changed in a way that meant deductions that had been planned over time and would be offset by future income and expenses were now due without any counter measures. But just the way it happened seemed inhumane and unjust.

And the IRS expected me to just write a check like I normally did to settle up. I hated to break it to them, but they couldn't get blood from a stone. That meant something had to be figured out, and if we couldn't come to an agreement, the problems would really mount. There was the prospect of court fights, judgments, and then if something possible wasn't worked out that really would open the door to late fees, delinquencies, garnished income, and charges that could lead to prison.

The deep feeling of uneasiness settled in as it seemed like my entire life could veer off course into nightmare territory that had previously been unthinkable. I wasn't the only one this was happening to around this time, and I'd heard stories of people being carted off to prison or had their lives torn apart. People were ruined because of this, and it could've happened to me. I had a wife and family to take care of, and failure was not an option.

So what did I do? Well, at first I tried to stick with my normal approach when it came to the IRS and personally do as little as possible. This went to the extremes in the form of me giving power of attorney to my CPAs so that they could deal with conducting a negotiation with the IRS in my stead. We'd brought up my aforementioned temper and loose tongue, and this was one situation where that was not going to help. The accountants would deal with it to the best of their ability within the bounds of my finances, and I'd sit back and accept the consequences.

At least that was how it was supposed to work out.

So here I was wondering how I was going to deal with this mountain of unexpected debt. Day after day, week after week passed, and the issue dragged on. The entire time I was stuck wondering what I owned that I'd have to let go of in a fire sale. My kids at the time were of high school and college age and needed help starting their lives. What was going to happen to them? I was trying to save for their college tuition, not to mention my own retirement. That all seemed likely to go completely out the window.

For some reason, the message from my CPAs was that the people at the IRS kept wanting to meet with me, which made no sense as far as I was concerned. My accountants and attorneys had complete control, and it wasn't like I wanted to make friends with the people who were trying to divest me of everything I had.

But it kept coming up. "No," I'd say. "Absolutely not. Tell them no. Seriously, it's not going to happen." I did not want to meet them. Giving them even just the time of day seemed like more attention from me than they deserved. But then my accountant told me that they actually wanted to help. Well, I found that hard to believe. And if they wanted to help, they could just do so through my accountants. I couldn't imagine how getting face to face with anybody was going to change anything.

With serious misgivings, I reluctantly agreed. The meeting was set, and I accepted the uncomfortable prospect that I'd be sitting down with people who spent their lives fleecing people on behalf of the Federal Government. In retrospect, it didn't go as badly as I thought, but I'd sure never want to be in a situation where I met with them again.

At the meeting, I met the agent from the IRS who was handling my case. As I said before, the agent was nice to the point of being gushing, like I was some kind of big shot. Who knows, maybe I was. For all I knew all anybody at the IRS did was sit around and talk about how the 1986 tax law had twisted things in such a way to leave me up to my ears in money owed.

After pleasantries were concluded, somewhat tepidly on my part, it turned out my accountant was right in that the agent I was meeting with did bring up something with the intention to help me. A lot of what drove the IRS agent's interest in meeting me was curiosity over why I didn't just file Chapter 7 bankruptcy to dispense with the debt and resolve the dispute. According to the agent, doing so would've eliminated roughly fifty percent of what I owed.

My accountants and I hadn't ever really discussed the prospect of declaring bankruptcy, so it was a novel idea that technically merited the meeting, and dropping the amount owed down to merely somewhere around $700,000 would've been nice, but I didn't waste any time letting the agent know that I wouldn't be doing that.

Why? There are downsides to declaring bankruptcy, such as a hit to creditworthiness and other financial hassles, but for me it boiled down to something simpler. Maybe it was something that came from being a small kid who had to stick up for himself, but declaring bankruptcy to me sounded a lot like admitting failure and giving up. It was fear of failure that drove me! It felt like I'd be saying I got in over my head and couldn't handle it. Yes, the rules had changed, putting me in a pickle, but I didn't want to spend the rest of my life having that hanging around my neck. I faced a tough situation, and running away from it wasn't how I wanted to be remembered.

When I told the agent definitively that bankruptcy wasn't for me, the agent somehow seemed even happier than previously. I guess that made sense—the agent's job was to secure outstanding funds owed to the government, and I'd just said beyond a shadow of a doubt that I'd reject alternatives that might provide me relief.

That was when the agent called me a phoenix, saying it with a smile and plenty of relish. I was familiar enough with the concept of this mythical bird but didn't see how it applied. It took me a minute to put the context together, and I have to admit it made me uncomfortable. Being called a phoenix by an IRS agent sounded like one of the most notorious monikers they had. It wasn't the scofflaws and cheats they had special names for. No, the people who had the perceived means and the value to deliver a fortune to Uncle Sam's coffers at some future time were the ones holding a special place in their imaginations.

Now that the meeting was in the rearview mirror, it was back to the negotiations. I never regretted my decision to forego declaring bankruptcy, and it eventually turned out to be a good choice. The negotiations started moving along in a way that seemed more fortuitous. The government had let go of the prospect of getting an immediate all-at-once payment, accepting that I simply couldn't do it, and they started working with a different payment mechanism.

I'm not sure how much the meeting played into it, but when I saw the deal they offered that I eventually accepted, the payment terms reminded me a lot of that concept of a phoenix and how it would relate to me. What ended up happening was that the IRS was going to give me a ten-year note to pay off the debt with payments of $400 per month and a balloon at the end.

In financial parlance, a loan with a balloon consists of an outsize portion of the debt that had to be paid all at once at the end of the loan term. Basically, these $400 per month payments would only cover roughly $48,000, and then the final payment would be a big old balloon of the remainder, in this case over $1.3 million.

This more or less gave me a ten-year window to earn the money I owed them, in one way or another. Considering what I was earning then, I'd be more or less working for the Federal Government to save up everything I brought in, with some room to spare, so that I could pay off this debt.

As daunting and unpleasant as this was, there were reasons why it was a good idea. I obviously hoped my earnings would grow over the next ten years to sufficiently cover this debt, but my assets would also rise in value over that time as well. It's pretty basic financial knowledge that money ten years in the future is worth a lot less than money today. To some degree, this was an offer providing some relief, even if it still meant forking over a huge amount of money. Also, I was afforded additional creditor protection by the IRS lien added to the protection of my irrevocable trust, which allowed me to aggressively negotiate settlements on my terms.

Perhaps there was a degree of leniency here on account of the abrupt and impossible-to-predict nature of these debts. After all, they could've come down hard on me and insisted that I pay straight away before they handed the matter over to their legal team, but it still meant money steadily draining out and that big balloon floating over my head for the next ten years. I was forty-six years old at the time as well, so I was getting into my peak earning years, and it looked like the IRS was going to be scooping up the lion's share of it.

The deal done, I got started making those $400 monthly payments. I can't say I blamed Ronald Reagan directly for the situation I'd found myself in, but I couldn't help but wish somebody had either never come up with this depreciation and deduction change in the first place or had taken it out before the tax bill got to its final draft. No doubt a liberal democrat who never held a private sector job, owned a business, or was at all entrepreneurial.

But there was nothing for me to do about it other than continue to make those payments. As time has a habit of doing, it continued on, with one month leading to the next. The years passed. Reagan left office. The '80s turned into the '90s. Other consequential things happened in my life, such as my bloody brawl with the banks that we'll be getting to next that also threatened to leave me without a penny to my name, and the whole time I knew the day would come when the term of my note to the government would expire, the balloon would descend, and I'd either be able to pay the balance all at once or try to negotiate the terms or I'd be in a heap of trouble.

Years continued to slip away. I got to work on developing the national independent insurance agency alliance model (SIAA). Now that you know more about my financial struggles here and what I had hanging over me, you can get the sense that for a lot of people this would've been a stressful situation. I couldn't afford for this not to work out, because I had huge personal but no business-related obligations notwithstanding the protection afforded by my irrevocable trusts.

This whole banking issue would stress most people. Actually, I enjoyed the gamesmanship toying with the simple, incompetent bank officers and their attorneys. I was never nervous because I knew that I was negotiating from a position of strength as my core businesses were doing very well and remained out of reach to my personal creditors.

I'd been in the insurance business long enough to be confident that this was the direction I had to be moving in. The strength of my team and our approach was going to be enough to carry this, I believed, and the only thing up in the air was whether it would provide to a degree that resolved the balloon.

We didn't exactly live a pauper's life over this ten-year period, but this deal with the IRS weighed over many of our family decisions, forcing us to forego things we otherwise would've done. I had a savings account designated for making contributions that would eventually go to the IRS at the end of the term, and if the amount in that account wasn't rising fast enough, I'd start to feel uncomfortable. I'm not the kind of person who goes into things unprepared, because the last thing I wanted to do was make things worse by not living up to my obligations. The chance to file for bankruptcy had long since passed, leaving me with nothing but the eventuality that I'd have to pay the final toll.

Or so I thought.

As the end of the negotiated ten-year term approached, the focus shifted from the $400 monthly payments, which now seemed like a pittance, to the massive final payment of well over a million dollars. That balloon, which started off far away, had spent the last decade inching closer and was now right up against me. Like the moon, it appeared small, but now that I was faced with the imminent prospect of having to pay it off, it appeared like a mammoth body.

I was ready to responsibly acquit my responsibilities, but the injustice of it all flooded back to me again. There was a whole heck of a lot I could do with this money if I didn't end up having to pass it over to the IRS, and it's safe to say that if I did then I wouldn't have many of the things I have in my life.

Then I got a call from my lawyer, who had checked in with the IRS about this to get some confirmation before the final payment became due. He had some startling news.

"The IRS didn't update the statute on your case," he said.

"So what does that mean?" I asked.

"It means you're off the hook."

I nearly fell out of my chair. Somehow this thing that had been hanging over me for a full decade was just gone, erased from existence, and all because someone at the IRS hadn't updated the statute, resulting in the limitations on the time allowed to pursue the debt to lapse. I sat back, my fingers over my lips, and marveled at it. That may be one of the best calls I've ever gotten in my life.

We were down to the very last month of the term, and it turned out that I'd even sent in my final $400 payment without needing to. I didn't fuss about it too much though. After all, I'd managed to cover a debt of $1.4 million with a scant $48,000 over ten years.

Now I can guess what you're thinking, that I didn't really "do" anything to make this happen. You might say this was a bonehead move on the IRS's part, or that I got off on a technicality, or that it was dumb luck. Maybe that's true to a degree, but I also put myself in position for this to happen. If I'd gone the bankruptcy route to cut my losses, that still would've ended up costing me over $650,000 more than I ended up paying in the end, not including legal and accounting fees, of course. I held out, I took responsibility, and I was able to reap the rewards when I finally caught a lucky break.

I do think it's worthwhile to read the tea leaves a bit on this one. This was most likely a simple twist of fate stemming from an oversight within the huge bureaucratic machinery of the IRS, but I'd like to think that somebody knew this was the right thing to do and consciously let the statute slip without updating it. Maybe that agent who met me at that one meeting decided that this actually was a wrongful case resulting from being unintentionally caught up in a provision of a new law, and that after ten years of payments and ten years of discomfort at having this hanging over me, I'd had enough.

From another perspective, this also seems like not only the appropriate outcome but also the one that should've been expected all along. You can't spend your life working in insurance without projecting those kinds of concepts onto these monthly payments and the balloon at the end. It just seems fitting that I was paying a $400 premium payment every month to protect me from the weight of this balloon. The proportions seem about right, $48,000 in payments to cover a $1.4 million dollar claim. It wouldn't be something I'd enthusiastically cover if it were my insurance company that had to approve the claim, but sometimes it pays to be the client. In this case, I think Uncle Sam has managed just fine without an extra million dollars from me, thank you very much.

No matter how you want to interpret this unexpected outcome, it would be an understatement to say that it was welcome to me. I felt like I'd hit the lottery (winning my own money) and was walking on air for days. It definitely was an occasion for a nice bottle of champagne.

Luckily, I'd just happened to save up enough for one.

As if handling all that wasn't enough, it just so happened that at the same time I was building the foundation for what would become a ten-billion-dollar insurance empire, a little something called the Strategic Insurance Agency Alliance. The SIAA model was extremely intricate and time-consuming to develop, and building it took years of my life, all the while these issues with the IRS and the banks threatened to destroy it before it could even be launched.

Let me tell you what happened.

chapter four

The Birth of SIAA

You really have to understand what it was I was doing and what I was trying to accomplish with my business. Without that, you won't have much of an idea of what I stood to lose. It's one thing to say that I owed a bunch of money to the government, and the banks were getting ready to sheer me. It's another to say that they were threatening the sustainability of a program that would put food on the table for thousands and thousands of people all across the country.

SIAA is something I consider my baby—it's what I spent thirty-eight years of my life creating, funding, building, and I couldn't be prouder of its continued success and the role I played in that. The leadership team has been excellent, and the entire model that I developed was innovative and highly entrepreneurial, but to even understand that, you have to have a firm sense of the state of the insurance market in the early '80s before this came along.

Back then, it was sort of like the Wild West when it came to insurance. Insurance was hardly a new concept—after all, even the Greeks and Romans had forms of insurance—but at that time rising asset prices led to insurance taking on a more prevalent role in society than it ever had before. Widespread growth in home ownership in the decades prior, the continued development of the banking system and mortgage markets, the evolving sophistication of automobiles, and the increases in the stock market all led to the rise of asset classes with prices that most people could not afford to replace and had to find a way to protect.

At the same time, you had dramatic inconsistencies in how insurance was being offered, often with results that would appear disastrous or unthinkable to us today. You had agents going door to door peddling life insurance and collecting weekly premiums.

This was when reputation and organization played a particularly key role, and I stepped into the industry and over the years found myself leading a medium-sized and sound agency in Keene, New Hampshire. As much as increasing sales was important, what I really focused on was creating a consistently performing methodology for operating a larger regional insurance agency with multiple divisions on a cross-sell basis.

We ended up doing well and were growing with sixty-seven agents working within our initial network known as the Satellite Agency Network (SAN). The goal was to grow more, but how best to do that posed a serious challenge. I was personally skeptical about the traditional ways to grow an agency business in this circumstance. Opening up branch offices in distant locations, hiring agency producers, or buying existing agencies meant overhead and the investment necessary. The other challenge was that Keene was fifty miles away from any similar population.

I hired Nick Pappajohn as my marketing director in 1984 and placed him in charge of SAN. Nick was a company marketing manager and was experienced in marketing insurance products, and I named him to be my second in command with a focus on building SAN. He then stayed with me for thirty-five years as we built out SAN and SIAA.

Attempting to purchase or buy out remote insurance agencies was a challenging way to scale, not just because of the capital-intensive nature of it, and of course the best targets were going to be the most reluctant about handing themselves over in a sale.

At the same time, I was firmly committed to grow outside of the traditional methods which were generally buying agencies, adding producers, and opening up remote branch offices. My plan allowed us to get paid to add to our growth. We knew we had put together a system that worked for sixty-seven independent insurance agencies, one that in many ways would be a structured business over how most other larger agencies were operating. We were hungry and motivated to grow, but doing so in a smart way is what makes all the difference.

Carrying the weight of bad agents or wading into tepid markets would throw our entire organization into jeopardy. The focus was squarely on allowing time for member agencies to sell insurance to grow their income and agency value, which also increased the income and value of SIAA. You could say SIAA (and SAN before) had to grow premiums, commissions, and overall value in order to receive its income. In other words, SIAA was all about performance, kind of like the three musketeers: "all for one and one for all."

Add to that how 1983 was what we in the industry refer to as a particularly hard market. Like much of the economy at the time, there were shock and contractions, and the insurance market wasn't at all spared. The whole thing was a mess. The underwriting grew particularly constricted, and you had instances where insurance companies in this sector were struggling, raising rates, and cancelling agencies or not agreeing to appoint any new agencies. Leverage was the key, and SAN was growing inordinately fast compared to the usual slight growth of the ordinary independent insurance agencies. And the insurance companies gave us appointments and other considerations that stagnant agencies were not exposed to.

I remember sitting at my desk, where I have a plaque (still) that reads, "In the middle of every difficulty lies opportunity." And as I did then and many times since, I'd sit there and stare at those words in an attempt to discover the opportunity in the difficulty. And that included creditor bank loans and the potential they offered. In this particular instance, I had the desire to focus on growing my agency by building a network of many independent insurance agencies that would allow us to leverage our combined size and significant premium growth in order to demonstratively improve the earnings and value of our member agencies and strategic company relations, unlike anything they could do on their own. And then to share ONLY in the growth in earnings and agency value. In other words, no growth, no SIAA income, or value.

There wasn't exactly a eureka moment, but I did come to realize that many of the other agents and companies out there that were struggling would've been doing much better if they'd simply been doing things the way our very successful model was doing them. I started pondering the idea of how we could extend our model to become an agency producer with smaller member agencies that were housed externally. This would solve a lot of the potential problems I'd been concerned about, allowing us to keep our overhead and risk low, all the while facilitating our reach into untapped markets and rural geographic locations but always away from urban areas.

I took charge of the idea and got to work on building a detailed "track to run on" that could become an attractive proposition to everyone, bumping up the margins so that we could cut in the external agents enough for them to do well, and so forth. It would follow the Masiello agency, which was doing very well and had great relationships with a focus on growth with our insurance companies. Solidifying the structure and creating the proper documentation for this was a monumental task, but I had incredible confidence in the likelihood of success, because it was what we'd already achieved with our own organization.

What we were going to be doing for smaller agents was to turn them into a BIG Agency by affiliating with SIAA—Big is Better. They didn't have to think about how to run an independent insurance agency. All they needed to do was integrate and assimilate our processes and stick to the program. And considering the persistent challenges in the market, this was going to be an attractive proposition for many. And of course for those trying to get into the industry by starting up somewhere, there was nothing for them.

That was the theory at least, the principle I was working under to develop a satellite agency network alliance, and I was lucky that the nature of the market continued to steer things in our direction. As we got closer to rolling out our model, the need for what I was planning only intensified.

In 1992-93, the national depletion of independent agents became a focal point of attention for the insurance industry as a whole. A consortium meeting of larger insurance company presidents took place in D.C. that year, and one of the attendees, the CEO of one of the top insurance companies and a friend of mine, was in attendance. When he got back to his office, he immediately gave me a call.

"You owe me a pair of pants," he said, and obviously I was flummoxed.

"I owe you a pair of pants...for what?"

He told me he'd meet me for lunch and tell me about it, and what he told me was that senior insurance company officers were convened by the national BIG I at their offices in DC, which was and is the national independent insurance organization. They'd just spent several days trying to figure out how to stabilize the market for independent agents, who were rapidly being forced out of business and leaving something of a vacuum in the market.

"They were all scratching their heads over how to fix this, and you're already doing that," he told me.

I was focused on developing a network in the northeast of New England, but if I could take it nationally, he told me, the opportunity was there.

"Alright, I'll buy you a pair of pants," I said.

It seemed easy enough, just take our successful SAN model and roll it out across the country. But that was naive on my part, and little did I know that it would never work and wasn't nearly as simple as that, not with so many different state regulations, licenses, companies, markets, and competitors. When I started to really look at what was going to be involved in a national rollout, it was enough to make me think maybe I was going to need another pair of pants, but I got down to work and started to figure it out.

Replication of the successful SAN model seemed like it would be easy. Wrong. There were reams of paper involved in fleshing out a national plan to contractually cover all our requirements, and what we realized we had to do was create a larger umbrella organization to cover not just our regional team but all the areas we wanted to get into, and that was the birth of SIAA. I remember spending large volumes of time pouring over national maps to determine the exact areas that we had named "exclusive territories." Dense urban areas were out, for example, because they had more consolidated markets with steeper competition and less room for smaller agents. That left smaller cities, towns, rural areas, and some suburban areas that we considered accessible and seemed like opportunity zones to us. I read Sam Walton's book (founder of Walmart) about strategizing preferred locations. One statement in Sam's book made the most sense to me: "Build it where they ain't." A lot of insurance companies did not want to spend their overhead marketing and appointing in smaller populations. That opened up all the other-than urban areas for development for SIAA. It made a lot of sense. The idea was to grow where competition was far less.

But as we got going, it became clear that clearing the regulatory hurdles and picking our spots was only half the battle. We still needed to reach larger regional agencies in these areas and convince them that it made sense to join SIAA as a Master Agency and to assimilate our best practices.

Our emphasis shifted to our marketing efforts. We needed a product of value to sell, so I took several months working with national maps to circle the urban areas, meaning we would leave those areas for the "big agents" and big companies. So, I created geographically located territories. We identified each list containing these prospects as an exclusive territory, about 500 in total each. My list focused on agency licensing per each state insurance department records across the country with the respective national insurance department.

The first person who joined us was Tom Barrett, someone I'd known for many years through Insurance Marketing and Management Services and other organizations. It took some convincing to get him to come over (three martinis), but he ended up taking a leap of faith that allowed us to achieve heights neither of us would've been able to reach on our own. So, in 1997, SIAA was rolled out nationally. Following Tom, we hired other Regional Presidents geographically.

Between my contacts and his, we now had access to a phenomenal number of larger regional agency owners across the country. He did an excellent job, knowing exactly what kind of message was going to resonate and how to get it out there. That was an important turning point that generated all kinds of interest but resulted in other challenging complications.

Having a lot of people in our target areas tell us they wanted to get on board and join SIAA was wonderful, but we knew enough to be careful about how we grew and who we agreed to let on board. Even though years and years had passed, many of the old problems about struggling agents and uncomfortable balance sheets remained. We wanted to help people develop a better system, but we still had to develop an extensive vetting process so that we were empowering the right people who could best take advantage of our model.

Our business plan was premised on appointing less than 10% of the prospects located in our National Master Agency Exclusive Territories. Only about one in ten made it through the appointment process, which started with a financial stability process, and then those with issues being dedicated, being professional, being organized, or those with personal issues conflicts or questionable histories didn't end up making it. Our mantra was **"quality, not quantity."** Every entity we brought on was someone we could feel good about carrying our banner, the kind of people who were committed to the role and who we sincerely wanted to see succeed. Again, the business plan was set up for easy assimilation of the SIAA model. It was still challenging. On many occasions, we would look at one another and simply state the obvious: "You can lead them to the water, but you can't make them drink."

And that brings us back to those many national meetings Nick, Tom, and I attended—we became road warriors! There were times where I wondered how this was all working out for our network of agents on the ground. That feedback was important, because if it wasn't working out for them and they weren't making money, we would have to tweak the model, and our team was very adept at that process.

I really needed an organized assistant to point me in the right direction. That was when my now wife of over twenty-two years Kathy joined me as my executive assistant, recognized by the entire organization as the go-to person when I was tied up. She made all the travel arrangements and schedules for our travel as well as made sure that I was pertinent relative to senior insurance company staff and member agencies. She also coordinated two national meetings a year with each over 350+ master agency and senior insurance company officer attendees.

I remember one time when Nick had a meeting scheduled with a couple of our early SAN agents after five years being with us, and I was completely sure they were going to complain about our overrides or some other aspect of the terms that would've meant they felt they were getting the short end of the stick. Instead at our meeting, the two agency owner partners made it clear they really just wanted to thank Nick and me for the opportunity to work together. They were making headway financially after we'd taught them how to write quality business, and the profitability was there enough that they felt like they were able to achieve their goals. This was a "thank you" visit. They had new offices, new cars, kids in college, and an upscaled standard of living.

Calls like that were what told me that we were able to strike the right note and achieve the kind of balance that we needed to where everybody was winning. We'd done it, the rest was history, and all we had to do was to remain focused to continue to carry out our model and work with our leadership team and Master Agency member agents. Our number of agents swelled to nearly five thousand, averaging over 450+ new member agencies for eight consecutive years. SIAA exceeded ten billion in insurance premiums, and it's continuing to have phenomenal success thanks to the leadership team led by my son Matt who had twenty-four years growing in all aspects of the system resulting in operations leadership and then succeeding me as CEO.

As I'm sure you've noticed, none of this happened overnight. This wasn't a get-rich-quick scheme or a good way to make a fast buck, but what it did do was create a system that continued to work over the long term, providing the kind of stability and seamless level of organization that many agencies lacked.

For me, a crucial component to our success and my personal success was my relentless focus on working together as a team to achieve results. When we had highly qualified and skilled people working on our SIAA management team, we were able to maintain a culture that eschewed the kind of hierarchies typically seen in national organizations. We were all hard workers heavily experienced with an intimate knowledge of the business and a determination to get things done, and we were able to leverage that to conduct our business without a typical power structure or emphasis on positions. We were truly a highly entrepreneurial organization with clearly defined concentrations—all spokes on a wheel that operated somewhat independently with compensation commensurate with results and with no income limits while operating independently.

Our mantra was "always do better today than you did yesterday, because you have more experience today." We were always learning, always adapting, and that resulted in a business style that was highly responsive and able to absorb shocks. I remember when the Covid pandemic hit, and I convened a teleconference with the leadership team to determine our response. My position was that this was going to be "business as usual"—change nothing. People were going to be relying more on insurance, not less. And the numbers verified that approach as we saw substantial growth during the pandemic period that followed. That plus the fact that we were rurally structured successfully addressed the pandemic favorably.

I think I surprised many within the organization when I announced that it was time for me to move on. There was still more gas in the tank, you could say, but I was eighty years old after all, and I could feel that making a change was the right thing to do. I'm sure everyone's familiar with the saying that if you love what you're doing then it's not work. Well, I loved what I did with SIAA, but I could see that it didn't need me and I didn't need it as much as before. The time arrived for me to say goodbye, and I left without any regrets.

What really allowed me to move on was the senior team with my son Matt as CEO and our long-term, highly qualified CFO Paul Labonte, CPA handling the purse strings, automation, and other financial areas. Their expertise and dedication helped me every day over those last few years. My confidence in them was bedrock deep, and there were many instances before I made my decision when it became apparent to me that this group of competent individuals would be just fine once I was gone. If that wasn't the case, who knows? Maybe I'd still be working on my baby till the day I passed on, "toes up," but as it is the company couldn't be in better hands.

The overwhelming sentiment I have when I reflect on my time at SIAA is a profound feeling of gratitude. It's the relationships I miss, and I'm deeply appreciative of all the people along the way who helped make this venture a tremendous success. We achieved more together than we ever could've done alone, and I'm thankful to the point of being indebted to those who gave their time, energy, and creativity to this company. You've made my life possible, and together we've changed a lot of other lives for the better as well.

Now some readers who are less familiar with the industry or perhaps even have a less favorable view of the role of insurance as a whole in society might be wondering what the big deal is. They might say, so you created a decentralized entrepreneurial model. So what? Who really cares? Yeah, you made a lot of money, but what kind of contribution is that really?

There probably aren't all that many skeptics out there except wannabe competitors, but imagining there were, I have a good answer for them. It starts with a story.

As I mentioned, I spent a lot of time out on the road visiting different national areas to meet with larger regional master agencies and their member agencies, promote the model, and build our presence. At some points there were just so many gatherings and faces and saying or hearing the same things over and over that it would be hard to keep track. One time I was in West Virginia having a conversation with a well-dressed man and he said something that caught me off guard.

"I just want to thank you for the incredible financial impact you've had on West Virginia," he said. Although I was used to people thanking me, usually it was on behalf of their families or agencies, and this man was saying I'd done something special for West Virginia. Why?

It turned out he was the secretary of state, and I looked over to my wife Kathy at other end of the head table and I found out that she was right there sitting and talking with the governor of West Virginia and his wife. I was taken aback. Here we had the highest elected officials in the state attending this meeting along with over 300 insurance industry relationships and independent insurance agents. A resolution was read by the Secretary of State thanking me, SIAA, and our Partner Master Agency for having such a big impact on the lives of a broad section of the West Virginia people who lived here.

Prior to that, the state of Governor of Kentucky proclaimed me as a "Kentucky Colonel" for contributing to the economic welfare of the state. That's what the mission of SIAA and the role of insurance at its best are all about. We're not doctors, but we play a role in saving lives. We're not bankers, but we manage the stability of people's finances in the face of catastrophe and accidents. We're not the police, but we help protect people and keep them safe. The kind of safety net that insurance provides does a lot to make the way we conduct modern society possible.

As for the kind of business we developed and the way it was structured, you've got to remember that this was the '80s and '90s and for the most part prior to the mass adoption of the internet. Brick and mortar stores in populated areas were in their heyday, and the general rule of business was that if you wanted to be somewhere you had to lease some office space and open up shop. Our model was based on member agencies working from low-profile locations while focusing on lists of insurance prospects that met certain criteria. But now you can see all kinds of businesses that are predicated on this kind of model. We really paved the way for that, serving as pioneers when it came to achieving a national reach without opening up thousands of offices or employing tens and tens of thousands of people.

Our model called for member agencies to identify quality insurance prospects and to proactively solicit their business. We did not support the concept of high-visibility locations as that took away from the quality aspect.

The SIAA model and its written premium and number of member agencies is still unequaled and has been ranked a distant 1st place in all insurance agency marketing models by Insurance Journal national rating criteria. Today, countless models have what might casually be called a fiefdom model like this, and the prevalence of that should only make our work proving the concept more impressive. I fondly call these organizations "wannabes."

So that's what made this an innovative approach. As much as I was trying to reduce risk and limit overhead, there was also substantial risk when it came to deploying an entirely new business strategy. My faith and optimism were rooted in my experience and understanding of our market conditions, allowing me to keep going for years to do the predatory work that was required to create, launch, and grow the SIAA model. There were countless failure points, and nothing in business is guaranteed to work out as planned. And then once something works out, there are no promises that it'll continue to work out over the long term. It would've been so easy for the regulatory hurdles to prove insurmountable or the agents to underperform or the marketing to be a wash.

That's the nature of business. Nobody owes you a living, and you have to get out there and earn it yourself. That being said, it helps to have a team with you. For me it always comes back to the fundamentals. Treat people well, be creative, welcome change, and outwork the competition. Use the data to make decisions.

In case it hasn't been made clear enough, I'm a little biased in favor of SIAA and the work that it continues to do, the outlook that it has, and the special opportunity it was to grow this entrepreneurial model from scratch into a great American institution. I firmly believe we were able to do things the right way, never compromising on our values, and that's led to a reputation of respect and dignity that is well deserved.

But as much as things went pretty smoothly, as anyone who's worked in business administration can tell you, that's no guarantee something won't arise externally to derail what you're doing. That's what happened to me several times, and as we're about to see it was no picnic.

Through even the toughest days, what I want to leave off here with is the sense that I knew I was lucky to be doing what I was doing where I was doing it and with whom, even though I knew it wasn't all going to be easy.

As I reflect on the SIAA story, I can truthfully say that my purpose was not to generate a highly valued business. My allegiance and focus was always to enable good people who wanted to be successful to do so taking advantage of our model.

From a personal standpoint, I think of the old adage "what doesn't kill you makes you stronger." I've been knocked down so many times, but that only allowed me to withstand a little more and push back harder once I got up. I kept trying to extend myself and in the process discovered I could do more than I ever thought possible.

chapter five

The Big Banks Come to New Hampshire

After reading about how grateful and cooperative I was with the team I worked with at SIAA, you may have gotten the impression that I'm always a nice guy who bends over backward to be respectful and doesn't hesitate to turn the other cheek.

Even the IRS agents were just doing their jobs and carrying out the letter of the law, admittedly a moving target where I was concerned. I couldn't fault them too much, and I never got the impression that they were motivated by personal animus, pure greed, or on a never-ending power trip.

My situation with the banks was a different story, and it should put to rest any mistaken impressions about what kind of person I am when someone's trying to step on my neck.

When working in the insurance industry and operating a leasing company, it's normal to have a complex relationship with not just one bank but many, involving lines of credit. That access to capital was important from a business perspective. I also had plenty of interactions with banks and credit from both a personal standpoint and from ventures that weren't related to insurance.

For example, for seven years I owned a pair of marinas in Kennebunkport, Maine, as well as a 36' boat I obtained for two hundred thousand that benefited from financing. I love the water, the seaside, and I had been spending time in the summer in Kennebunkport for seven years after relocating from Wells, ME.

The important thing to note is that through all this, my relationships with the banks have been beyond friendly. I knew a lot of bankers in the area and was friends with them, but more than that they all wanted to do business with me. Whatever plans I showed up with, they saw them as an opportunity to make money and didn't hesitate. There was never a late payment and certainly never a default. It was a seamless relationship no matter which door I walked into, and I benefited from having the access to financing for whatever I felt like doing or whatever the business's needs were.

That all changed in the early 90s. This was a period of consolidation in the banking industry around the northeast, and suddenly the friendly and helpful guys I'd been working with for decades were replaced by cold, calculating guys from regional or national banks that had bought up our local banks as promoted by the RTC.

Now, whether the bankers were friendly or icy shouldn't have mattered much. After all, my credit was sterling, everything paid on time, and the banks earned boatloads on the interest from our loans, but their demeanor extended to the way they performed their jobs, and it came with disastrous results.

As soon as these takeovers happened, notices started going out about denied loan applications, cancelled extensions, and calls for payments that weren't due. And I'm not just talking about me. I mean statewide in New Hampshire. Suddenly businesses were being forced to close on a catastrophic scale because they couldn't make payroll, fund purchase orders, or cover loan repayments in full.

I can't say I know exactly why these banks suddenly took such a hard stand, but I have some guesses. These larger banks bought the distressed local New Hampshire banks for access to their capital and deposit slips so that they could fund larger loans, usually in their home territory. Obviously, it didn't help them if a substantial portion of their new funding was distributed through small- and medium-sized loans, and so they started to cull those aggressively.

That meant small businesses and startups bore the brunt of this wave, and the banks, such as Fleet bank, were unyielding in the face of any pleas for mercy. The pain this caused on a personal level was profound as people lost their livelihoods, their businesses, or their jobs because the place they worked at had to fold. And as I knew from experience, these were not dispassionate business decisions that nonetheless were above board.

Let me tell you a story about my boat. Now I don't want to name names or try to shame people thirty years after the fact, but you tell me if this is how a bank should try to do business.

I was working on obtaining a bank loan to pay off the boat. A bank loan officer came to see me in my office. He requested that I personally guarantee the note I was requesting on behalf of the boat loan. When I refused, he said it was fine based on my credit and bank relationship but had me sign the line calling only for the Kennebunkport Marina as borrower.

The Marina owner that I was buying from called to tell me the loan had been approved and that was that. I thought the boat note was co-signed by the Marina owner as part of the sale process or that the bank had dropped their position for my personal guarantee.

After a couple of years with the boat note performing, we had a demand for payment in full on the balance of the loan. There was one other alternative—they also would accept my boat, sell it, and I would be responsible for the balance due. My eyes narrowed. I told the bank that in no way was the signature on the loan application mine.

I had no choice but to say goodbye to my boat, and the bank advised me that they would sell the boat, and that I'd be responsible for the balance after applying the funds from the sale.

Lo and behold, I then got a demand for the balance of the note. It looked like the boat had sold for a piddly amount and I was going to get stuck paying the difference. We all grew incredibly suspicious, and we asked the bank who the buyer of the boat was. For some strange reason, they refused to tell us, but that was something we could fix. Our next move was to issue a court order for disclosure. Can you guess who might've bought it?

You won't be shocked to hear it was an officer of the bank, and the sale price was nowhere near market value.

Our cries of indignation were met with a swift rejoinder. The bank took us to court and produced the executed note that had my signature on it, meaning that I was after all responsible for the difference no matter who bought the boat or at what price. But wait a second, I'd refused to sign the note loan application, and yet here I was looking at the same document with my name attached like I'd whipped out a pen and put my name to it. Had I stepped into the Twilight Zone?

No, this was fraudulent behavior on another level, and we hired a handwriting expert who convinced the court that my signature had been forged. The end result? The judge chewed out the bank for bringing the suit against me and tossed out the bank's case. I didn't get the boat back, but the loan balance of about $60,000 was gone, about the best I could hope for.

But resolving the loan wasn't the last word in this story.

As we were leaving the court proceeding, the bank's attorney started walking toward me in a menacing way. He was 6'5" and was uttering threats about what he was going to do to me and insults that I couldn't in good conscience reproduce here. I didn't back down and instead looked him square in the eye and said, "Screw you," which nearly sent him over the edge. His being a lawyer was barely enough to keep him from taking a swing at me. His last words were, "This is not over!"

Sometimes the biggest guys are the smallest people.

That might have been the most egregious example, but there were plenty of others that came close. And in a very short time span my banks went from being a big catalyst for my growth to an incredible hindrance that threatened everything not secured by irrevocable trusts and of course the IRS Lien. In 1991, it was like my money dried up. I couldn't get any new loans, my existing lines of credit were frozen, and then the existing loans I had started being called. By 1992, banks' attorneys were taking me to court in an attempt to get every dollar they could back pronto. Suddenly I was in deep. However, the operating companies that I had established in an irrevocable trust a number of years earlier could not be touched by creditors in addition to the IRS Lien, which took precedence. So, there was not much to get except whatever discounted amounts the pledged asset had. So, each situation stood on its own, which made our negotiations very favorable. What the banks did not want anyone to know was that when they were shuddered by the RTC, they discounted most notes, so whatever was collected in the future would be booked as profit for earnings and compensation bonuses in a number of situations.

You have to realize that even successful, profitable businesses were being wiped out because of strong-arm tactics to repay large loans all at once without much warning at all. Like other businesses, our cash flow just could not accommodate a repayment of this size. And it wasn't like anyone could go to another bank for help, because they were all behaving like this.

Don't forget that I was still making my monthly payments to the IRS, and the balloon was slowly getting closer. Unable to see the future, I had no idea the statute of limitations would run out and instead figured that the banks would pulverize me only for the IRS to show up at the end to scrape off the scraps.

During this process, my operating companies were doing well, and the SAN Group of agencies was thriving. The glaring difference between the issue with the IRS and these banks was the scale. Owing $1.4 million to the IRS was daunting, but the insurance agency, travel agency, and real estate sales entities were in a trust that could not be subjected to my personal debt or the IRS Lien. The amount of debt being called by these banks was a full tenfold that. By the time we sorted out where we stood, we calculated that we were being forced to repay $14 million.

Hemorrhaging that amount of money would've had catastrophic consequences. Our insurance agency and other operating companies owned in trust plus the IRS Lien gave me plenty of leverage to negotiate as they could not be touched by creditors. Without the operating entities, bankruptcy would've been unavoidable, and with it would come that acknowledgement or failure and defeat I'd been so adamant against.

When I met with my attorney and CPA, we discussed strategy. My attorney said that "you are personally insolvent." That meant that the trust owned the core businesses and had nothing to do with any bank loans. Also, we were reminded that there was no way any creditor on personal loans or other than trust loans (there were none) would have access to the core businesses. Hmmm—that sure changed my negotiating tactic. In reality, I could have just walked away from the loans and the collateral value and told the banks to stick them.

Meanwhile, the pressure to resolve this continued to climb. I was hounded by calls day and night telling me to pay up. They were telling me I'd need to cough up the entirety of the balances on term loans that were in conformance. But I needed to be able to draw additional funds to continue to fund the projects underway. When pushed, I simply told the banks, "Screw you. You can kiss my ass."

There was no point holding back my language, because they were already doing their worst to me. They expected me to fold, to break, to succumb to their demands like all the other NH businesses that were history.

They weren't used to people standing up for themselves, and I was about done being pushed around.

The mandatory meetings continued, although I would decide which ones that I would attend, much to the chagrin of the banks, leading to nasty exchanges that kept getting worse and worse.

One of the loans was for the purchase of a Motel in Kennebunkport. The bank had agreed to provide $45,000 as a loan to convert a restaurant to rooms from summer operating profits. That would have been on top of a $1,400,000 mortgage.

A bank chairman and friend warned me about the new president assigned by the successor bank to "clean up" the NH bank issues and agreed to meet with me. When I got to his office, the first words out of his mouth were, "Here's what you owe. Pay it."

"I don't have the money," I said for the umpteenth time, and he decided this was a good segue into unusual territory for a meeting like this.

"Let me tell you what I think about your state," he said. Oh boy.

And there I *was* sitting in a meeting and being forced to listen to this banker in a suit trash talk New Hampshire. It didn't go down well, but this banker didn't care and definitely didn't hold back from sharing the full extent of his contempt. I'd had enough.

"Let me tell you something. You may think you're Goliath, but guess what? I'm David," I said.

He lowered his eyes at me, not amused by the analogy.

"You're no David," he said, and I gave him a look. I then reminded him of the biblical story of David and Goliath as I walked out the door and told him, "Say goodbye, David, because I'm going to have your ass!"

Is it too much of a spoiler to say that he'd eat those words?

Part of his disdain for NH was because he did not want to be there. He had received three speeding tickets in his red Porsche driving between Providence, RI and Manchester, NH, or so he said!

My lead council at the time was a former congressman and good friend whose campaign for office I worked previously. We got together to try to pin down our response. We'd been insulted, harassed, and threatened. Simply fending them off and avoiding insolvency wasn't good enough any longer. We wanted to make them pay for what they'd done.

That meant bringing the fight to them, so we put together a lawsuit against the bank, the likes of which they'd never seen. There were five counts against the bank, and each count required a jury trial. This bank was responsible for a number of small NH businesses folding so the idea of trial by jury would have cost them a ton of money and further damaged its horrendous reputation. This was going to be a monstrous legal entanglement for even the biggest bank, and the exposure they had for huge legal bills wasn't even the lynchpin of this whole thing. The bank had an internal appraisal (joke) of the property that reduced the value by over fifty percent. The court hearing was over the fact that they bank stepped in and took possession of the motel and wanted the difference in settlement. I told them, "See you in court." I asked a favor of a professional appraiser that I had helped get several jobs to provide a "market appraisal." When we showed that to the judge, the bank took great exception but to no avail. The judge said, "I know how this works, as I am unfortunately used to this tactic."

I would have a difficult time devising a more perfect villain in a story for a circumstance like this than Fleet bank. The very way they conducted business that caused this kind of colossal problem for me was what made it possible for me to overcome them. Think about it. They'd been putting people out of business up and down the state of New Hampshire since the government stepped in, making them easily the most-hated institution in the state. You could not find a dozen people here who were unaffected by their carnage or had a positive opinion of them.

We were forcing them into not just one jury trial but five. They were stunned and didn't know what to do. We were waiting to enter the court when a group of judges were returning to the court from lunch. Three out of four judges were friends, and I had vetted them for Governor Sununu for their appointments to the bench. We exchanged pleasantries while the bank's attorney from Boston and the bank loan officer who was nasty during prior contacts watched.

I'll never forget that trip to court when the judge heard our case. This was an Attachment hearing. This was the judge that I did not know. He allowed me to take the stand so my attorney could have me respond to questions. In attachment hearings, this is not usually allowed. I took the stand and explained what happened and what we'd been going through. These attempts to call back loans early weren't just wrong. They were illegal.

After all had been said on our end, and the bank had a chance to make their case for why they were entitled to extort money from individuals and businesses in such a manner, the judge turned to me.

"Mr. Masiello, do you know the retirement age for a superior court justice?" he asked.

I replied that I didn't.

"It's seventy," he said. "So you can spend a few more years on that stand if that's what you'd like to do—all the way up until I retire."

A bittersweet moment came when the judge dismissed the bank's attachment of the motel and instructed the bank to turn all operations back to me.

You could see the blood drain from the faces of the bank officers and the Boston attorneys. The judge was giving us a free pass to spin our wheels at the bank's expense long into the future, allowing me to completely circumvent the burden of the debts related to these loans, and he all but tipped his hand about who was at fault and which way this case would go.

Just to add fuel to the fire, as the hearing was winding down, my attorney presented the court with a five-count trial by jury claim on my behalf. The expression on the faces of the bank attorney and officer was priceless! It was a huge relief to me, because I could count on the word of the judge, but this led to yet another vitriol-filled exchange once we left the courtroom. The banker from Fleet and his attorneys had swallowed the daunting pronouncement from the judge and regained their insolent demeanor.

"You haven't heard the last of me. I'll get your ass," he promised.

I just laughed.

"Bigger guys than you have tried—screw you."

All they had left were bluster and bluffs in the hopes that I'd cave in some way, but I was way beyond that. I was in control, the finish line was in sight, and I could get there whenever I wanted and still win.

There were a few more motions and things that followed, but it was clear the fight had gone out of them, and the prospect of the costs for a protracted and hopeless court battle started to look bigger than what we actually owed them. Eventually we reached a settlement that ended our suit and freed me from that debt. I subsequently had a buyer for the motel in Kennebunkport who had $800,000 and wanted the property. I met with the arrogant banker in his office and asked if he would accept $800,000 in exchange for the $1.4 million owed on the note. And that the Bank could not give me a 1099 or W-2 tax form. He agreed. So that was another $600,000 of forgiven debt. A little humor—because I was personally insolvent, the 1099 and W2 were unnecessary.

Now I'm not going to pretend that a handful of banks fully walked away from $14 million, bringing it down to nothing, but we did get big discounts and some serious breaks. Their tune changed pretty quickly, putting an end to the hardball tactics and bloodthirsty, predatory attempts to recover the debt. Extensions and the usual banking behavior that we expected from our financial partners on these loans resumed, albeit begrudgingly in some cases.

But the bigger message was that small businesses in New Hampshire shouldn't and wouldn't be victimized in this way, and that's an impact I'm proud even now to have helped deliver. Our case put every single bank in the state and in the region on notice that attempting to bait and switch terms or rake people over the coals for loans that were called early was not a smart move. If these banks had other priorities they wanted to focus on, they were just going to have to wait until the loans they'd already made expired in their natural course of time to be able to do that.

For me, there were some costs in all this that weren't fully accounted for in this surprising victory. Every bank operating in the region and New Hampshire was familiar with who I was, and on plenty of occasions I got the impression that the guys sitting down at the other end of the table were stricken with worry over the possibility that I'd drag them to court over the smallest little thing. There were some who outright hated me and wouldn't work with me. In plenty of cases that was fine, and those people could take a hike, but in others the value of the institution meant taking the time to rebuild trust and work together.

Fortunately, there were plenty of compelling reasons for banks to want to work with us, and none of them had to do with how much anyone liked me personally. I liked to let our balance sheet do the talking, and it was easy for me to sit there with a deadpan look and ask them if they wanted to get paid their interest and closing costs or if they wanted to fret about what happened to some knuckleheads when they let push come to shove.

Many of these banks were interested in rehabilitating their images too. No matter what they personally thought of New Hampshire, there were a lot of people doing business there, not to mention a robust legal system that had their backs, and trying to treat everyone within state lines like they were second-class citizens was going to cost these banks dearly. The era of bank consolidation and high pressure on local small businesses came to an end not a moment too soon.

For me, of course, this coincided with the success of the SAN Group and the beginning of the development of SIAA and our own push to stretch beyond our area into the national scene. Yes, the banks were in check and terrified of crossing me again, which meant our business was secure and my personal finances were going to be in a good place for when the IRS balloon popped, though it was unknowingly only full of hot air. But the experiences I had with these banks getting into new territory was very instructive for me as well.

In all these cases, the RTC brought banks into New Hampshire looking at what they could extract from the region and take home. They didn't care about any of the businesses and people in New Hampshire or what they needed, and that led to a rude awakening down the line. It couldn't have been more glaring to me that we needed to do things a different way, focusing on the partnerships and the value that we could add for our member agents and their families and communities. If I couldn't look in the mirror and tell myself with a straight face that the impact we were going to have would be positive, then we couldn't do it.

And that saved me a few times. After spending several months writing the agreements, our contractual terms were clear with the sole purpose of ENABLING our new agents and existing agencies to be able to increase their income and value. It would've been so easy to just say, OK, let's hold onto a little more and they'll be alright. Then those calls and gatherings with agents and their families might've turned out quite differently. My concepts were based on many little things add up to a lot. It was tricky designing and writing member agreements that provided that SIAA would be paid membership fees that were based solely in growth of each member agency, so we had to perform. I plagiarized several well-known "franchise agreements," but in each instance, I had legal counsel advising me how not to be a franchise. So, the cash flow was tight building the model, but as more agencies joined, the cash flow reflected that.

It didn't escape me that if we'd been looking for more in fees there could've been another Jim Masiello out there on the other side of our equation with a good lawyer and a sense that he was David fighting against ourselves in the role of Goliath. It only takes wronging one person to usher in a cascade of problems that can severely hamper even the strongest institution, but we never had a problem with anyone.

For fun, try Googling "SIAA lawsuit." You won't find anything even remotely pertinent to us, because there's nothing there, and as long as the leadership team keeps running the company with the lessons they have learned in mind, there won't ever be.

When I reflect on all that happened to me up through the turn of the century—the development of SIAA, the collision with the IRS, and having to fight off these banks—I'm left with a feeling of awe about how it all turned out.

If I rolled the dice one hundred times, I don't think it would've turned out like this again, probably not nearly as well. The only thing that got me through was the grit and fighting spirit I grew up with. Back on the streets in our neighborhood, I never learned how to give up, and all of my experiences were continuing to pay off for me.

I find it humbling to consider where I might be and what might've happened if things had gone differently, but perseverance became our mantra. What if SIAA hadn't taken off and instead run aground, and if I'd had to shell out the million dollars plus for the balloon to the IRS and if the banks? I was in a strong position thanks to our irrevocable trust, but there were still dramatic consequences possible looming over me for years. People in similar situations were sent to prison or had their homes taken away. The risk to my family was real, and I tried to shield them from having to contend with what the fallout might be.

I remain ever thankful for an attorney friend of mine who, over a couple of martinis, pushed me to use my vision of success long term by creating my irrevocable family trusts to own the businesses.

If any of that had not been the case, would I still be as tough about it as I was as a kid growing up in a poor neighborhood? Would I still hold my head up the way I do now? Would my family love and respect me the same?

I'd like to think the answer would be unequivocally yes to all those questions, but the honest truth of it is I'm not so sure. There are a lot of people out there who've worked just as hard and perhaps harder than I did and didn't end up doing nearly as well, some of whom have had challenges and difficulties that while different might be comparable. I have no doubt my family would stand with me through anything and see me as more than just my job or my paycheck, but I can't escape the truth that those things do mean something to me.

All I can do is accept the hand that I've been dealt and, considering how it's gone, be incredibly grateful for it.

chapter six

My Saga with Banks Continues!

Y ou may think all that would be enough trouble with banks to last a lifetime, and you'd be right. But for me it was just a drop in the bucket. I can't for the life of me tell you why. Maybe it's something about my face or appearance that invites people to act this way, or being in the insurance profession makes people think they can push me around, that I'd just lay down and play dead.

Then they have to learn the hard way that's not the case.

As I mentioned, I've been involved in a number of pursuits, and that includes real estate, commercial leasing, the largest travel agency in the region, and land development and construction which can often make for a very good investment and also comes with the perk of being able to use the places you're working with. Being where I was in New Hampshire, there was a lot of pristine land around with untapped potential, and in the

'80s and '90s, having the Boston and New York crowd come up during the summers was something we could reliably bank on, figuratively and literally speaking.

I became aware of a large tract of land around a small lake called Mendums Landing, which is smack dab between Concord and Portsmouth, NH. Beautiful place with the kind of picturesque scenery that New England is known for, and although it's far smaller than Lake Winnipesaukee, that only made it more exclusive. Its more southerly location made it easier to get to, less of a drive, and closer to the amenities of civilization.

As if that weren't enough, the land was originally owned by Robert Frost, one of America's preeminent poets, best known for poems like "The Road Not Taken" and "Stopping by Woods on a Snowy Evening." He also wrote a famous poem called "Mending Wall," which to me sounds like a reference to Mendums Landing and just happens to be about staking claim to territory and setting boundaries between us. What a coincidence.

The famous line from that poem is "Good fences make good neighbors." But what about when no one's had a chance to put up a fence yet? Well, I was about to find out.

In case you haven't already guessed, I was licking my chops over this piece of land and ready to make it a very special development. A beautiful spot by a lake with a famous pedigree in the middle of Vacationland, New Hampshire? The opportunity couldn't get more obvious that this was a jackpot waiting to happen, as close to a sure thing as there is on this Earth.

I met with the owner about buying the property, but he didn't prove to be as willing and eager as I'd been led to believe. Maybe he knew what he was giving up, but he was fully aware he wasn't going to be doing it himself, so over many meetings and a long period of time I finally was able to engineer the sale of the property to our development company for a high-end low-density development in part to protect a large loon population that did not allow structures within seventy-five feet of the water.

Despite the squandered time, the belief that rich tourists or people transplanting into the area would eat this up kept me going. I imagined people lining up for this and the closings to stretch long into the night. Well, it wouldn't be that easy.

To pay for all this, I went to a local NH bank in the hopes that this would be the kind of comfortable transaction with the good old boys I was used to. This particular bank was one that had courted me in the past for a relationship with my companies, but the stars had never aligned, and we'd never actually worked together. As a matter of fact, in reality, I was never impressed with their competence. However, considering how eager they were, I was sure there'd be no trouble at all—little did I know.

I laid out a proposed financing arrangement whereby we structured the loan around a lot release payback net of developmental costs. So, each time a lot sold, the profit margin would go to repaying the loan. Once the loan was paid off, the remaining lots would then sell and constitute our profit margin. And if one lot happened not to ever sell and I had to keep it for myself, well, these things happen and having a new heavenly vacation property would be the burden I'd have to bear.

The first thing I did was hire a land planner and forester to prepare the subdivision and create a master plan for the parcel. We landed on a minimum lot size of five acres with only one residential home allowed per lot with certain additional restrictions. This density seemed like the right tradeoff that would maximize our investment. The other key stipulation was that there could be no cutting of trees within seventy-five feet of the water. Also, no fossil fuel boat motors were allowed. Had to keep the pond looking good, loon population intact, and people wouldn't want to go there as much if it was ringed with multi-story waterfront houses.

So, we met at the site with the planner and forester. There was a dirt road into the site, which was the only way in. I had been forewarned that there was a disgruntled abutter but did not know of his desire not to allow anyone to use the access dirt road, even though we had rights to full access and use. We drove in, and not far ahead there stood this hermit right in the middle of the road holding a rifle. He was not about to move for us, and the look in his eye said it all.

"So, what do you fellas want?" were the first words he uttered.

I told the others to stay in the car and got out and introduced myself. I said "Hi, I'm Jim Masiello, and I own the Frost property, so we need to pass."

He said, "Get your ass off this property. This gun is loaded, and I will use it."

I absolutely believed him. Clearly this was not the time to argue, so I got back in the car. We eventually had to have the local police accompany us onto the property. Our disgruntled buddy was told to put his gun away and to get out of the way of anyone passing his property—a real woodsy shit hole!

We got all our approvals in place and started to market the lots. Everything was going great and shaping up nicely when suddenly out of nowhere we got word that our project was being shut down. RTC, the Resolution Trust Corporation, which was a government-owned asset management company handling the sale of five NH banks to larger out-of-state banks, real estate-related assets during this time, was leaning on the NH banks to pull the plug on the loan and the project.

Once again, I was shocked and in disbelief that this venture was in peril. Land development was as commonplace and mundane as it gets, and yet this had attracted some little incompetent government bureaucrat scrutiny and looked like it was going south. There wasn't as much room to fight here, since if someone says we couldn't divide the land, then we wouldn't be able to do it without the proper permission, but we did have an approved subdivision.

Because of pressure from the RTC, our bank called the loan, meaning that I was in the uncomfortable position of having paid the land costs and development costs without yet receiving the profits. There was no way I could just turn around and give them all their money back, and they knew it.

But I knew some of the officers at this bank. In fact, I knew every single member on the board of directors, and I started angling for a way out of this without losing my shirt. Usually when you have an issue with a bank, the way it's handled is through phone calls and letters. Unusually in cases like these, they invited me to meet with the entire board of the bank.

So, I showed up to the meeting with the board of directors with smiles and handshakes but ready to unleash the wrath of Jim just in case it became necessary. The bank's attorney wasn't present but participated via a conference call line instead. It rubbed me the wrong way that he couldn't be bothered to show up in person, but he and I had a very contentious meeting just before this event. Then things got worse as the board members began to demonstrate their incompetence by discussing the project.

Although nobody said it aloud, I clearly understood that several of these board members had it in the back of their minds that they wanted a piece of this project, and servicing a loan was not nearly going to cut it for them. These were bona fide jealous assholes who were probably more the problem than the RTC and were looking for a way to sink this project just because they could.

Calling a loan I couldn't repay would've nicely led to a foreclosure and taking possession of the property for them, and then they could've done whatever they wanted. I highly doubted the RTC would've harped on them about a subdivision of this quality and prominence.

More often than not, this has been the kind of experience I've had when trying to innovate and do business. I put in the legwork to do something new, and then somebody else will think the quick and easy road to success would be just to take it from me. It reminds me how if you have a bunch of crabs in a bucket, none of them will ever be able to climb out because they'll always have others holding on and pulling them back with their claws. These board members were my crabs, and they were holding me back out of jealous spite. My blood was starting to boil, and the conversation started to get intense with accusations and demands. I couldn't understand why they wouldn't just stick with the loan they had made.

At one point I was asked to go sit in the president's office to wait while they deliberated about what to do and what they would consider as a way out.

As I was approaching the office, I overheard the bank attorney on speaker phone with the President advising that the bank had better work out a satisfactory resolution with me because the bank was vulnerable due to their other commitments and obligations plus the scrutiny of the RTC and the last thing they should do is get it to a community-wide public dispute with me.

Even after I came out, the discussion didn't seem to go anywhere, but the bank attorney, still on speaker phone, was the first one to grasp that the bank did not want to go down this road playing hardball with me until there was only one of us left standing. Although I knew these board members—wasn't close friends with them, but I knew them—only the bank attorney seemed to grasp the significance of who they were dealing with. He said they were a community bank, and I was not one to get into a battle with. Maybe he'd done his research on me and knew how our lawsuits with other banks had gone. He also might've just had an idea of how connected I was in the community. A few words from me, and these guys could've had quite a few withdrawals and account closures the next day.

Despite all that and the bank's own attorney telling the board of directors to turn tail and run, the meeting ended without a satisfactory offer or a resolution. They wouldn't budge, and I finally said I'd had enough and was going to leave. There's only so long you can sit in a conference room with stupid, incompetent people who vehemently disagree before you realize that you're going nowhere.

It was starting to look like I was going to have no other options than to pay up or walk away as there was no way the bank could collect from an insolvent borrower. Surprisingly, I got a call at home from the bank's board chairman with a third option. He said the bank would set up a payback schedule in which every dollar I paid them would reduce the debt on the loan by two dollars. They were willing to take a 50% loss on the loan, but they sure wanted that remaining fifty percent.

As I considered this, I realized it was a mixed blessing and still carried some risk. Yes, the outstanding amount on the loan then was $1,150,000, and suddenly I would only need to pay back $575,000. It was hard to imagine getting a better result going to court or continuing to press them, but at the same time I was not in position to be writing a check for that amount either. I would not take money from my profitable operating companies to repay any external personal debt that I was not responsible for. I was adamant with the bank that any agreement would have to be assignable by me under these terms and conditions.

I could see the kind of trap they were weaving. A judge wouldn't look favorably on me if one heard I'd received a sweet deal like this and still stuck my nose up at it, but there was still only one way to raise that kind of money, and it wasn't one that I felt great about. I'd have to sell the property expeditiously and perhaps at less than market value or else once again face the risk of foreclosure.

I let them sweat a few days and then called the Chairman and said I would take the deal conditioned only on sales either of the project in its present status or the sale of the first lot and that these conditions would continue until the note was paid and I would have no further expense or liability. They took the deal. What I did not tell them was that I had a buyer developer who was hyperventilating over the thought of owning what had become known as Frostlots.

Considering all that we'd been through, our grand plans with our development company were shrinking rapidly, we wanted to scale back our activity, and I wasn't eager to keep going in this direction when the rug could get pulled out from under me at any time.

It took some more negotiating with the development company, but I was able to get a deal that worked out tolerably well overall. The planning, approval process, surveying, and foresting work I'd put in was valued, and I was able to get out at roughly even with the bank still getting their $575,000.

In some ways I'd dodged a bullet, but it was still of course well short of what I'd been dreaming of, and there was certainly not going to be a lot near the lake left over for me. At least a bank board member wasn't able to grab it for a steal and gloat to me about his Robert Frost Snowy Woods development.

Sometimes the best we can hope for is to get out with our shirts and grab the first lifesaver available before the ship sinks.

As for the bank, they have their own way of dealing with situations like these, which always strikes me as a little dubious. My supposition is that on their end they immediately wrote down most of the loan as bad debt, taking a deduction for it as soon as possible. Then when they get a windfall, such as the $575,000 I handed over in a nice lump sum, they immediately report that as income for their quarterly reports, allowing them to make the argument that they were profitable and that the bank was operating successfully so bonuses would be paid.

I've taken accounting classes in college and spent plenty of time in our accounting departments, so I know the gray areas and the ways rules can get bent, and it's just a wonder to me that the banks are able to work the numbers in this way and get away with it. This bank didn't have a profit of $575,000; that was the amount of their loss. And after what they put me through, I have some discomfort that they were probably able to spin this into a nice story for themselves. It's likely the only reason they made their offer in the first place, because they knew they could make it look better than it was.

Oh well. That's just one of my gripes and something I'd have changed if I was ever in charge of writing tax bills—along with plenty of other changes I could imagine—but I didn't have a chance to dwell on this long. The next inconceivable issue and heated confrontation were doubtlessly right around the corner.

Although SIAA proved to be excellent idea and a huge success, not everything worked out so spectacularly. Take Best Lease, a company we formed to provide loans for businesses to acquire expensive equipment plus the certificates of insurance covering the equipment.

It wasn't a complicated business model. Businesses and manufacturers had substantial equipment and machinery that they were leasing in order to carry out their work, and proof of insurance was required for the duration of the leases. It looked to us that we could generate additional insurance premiums and commissions by creating an entity focused exclusively on this requirement.

Once we began going down this path, we quickly found ourselves inclined to try to maximize the opportunity by taking on the entire process, not just handling the certificates but serving as a lending source for leasing commercial equipment, some of which easily cost thousands of dollars.

Some of these would be on the scale of what you might expect, except the assets were tucked away in warehouses, workshops, and manufacturing centers for sales and distribution. Looking back, we were renting a sizable advertising and marketing/office space in our building. The owner and operator was also a friend. He came to me one day and told me about a German printing machine that if he could afford would be very profitable.

I turned it over to our senior vice president in charge of Best Lease to set some credit lines up allowing us to set up leases for this purpose. We got the purchase of the loan approved, the lease in place, and of course the certificate of insurance. Our first lease as described was the German printing machine for $96,000.

The trick to doing this though was going to be securing the capital to make the loans, which means we'd be borrowing from a more traditional lender, one who would have to be willing to take the equipment as collateral and advance the funds to Best Lease, which would in turn assign all ownership rights and the Best Lease co-signature.

Yes, this made the business model quite a bit more complicated, but the opportunity for profit would theoretically increase as well. We markup the interest loans and pass them along to the customer, while being able to quickly handle the insurance aspect ourselves within our own network insurance companies. Killing two birds with one stone promised to give us a significant competitive advantage and degree of efficiency.

The first step was to find and on-board an experienced leasing person to head up this opportunity, which was always the way I operated. We found our person in short order, as this was a great opportunity, plus our compensation and equity offer was very appealing.

We had a bank take us up on the venture, and in no time flat we had ourselves our first customer and arrangement for our first piece of leased equipment, which happened to be the German printing machine.

Going through the process we just described, once the client vetted the machine for quality and became committed to obtaining it for the business, we then took the note signed by the business owner to the bank for an advance so that we could then enter into an installment note with the business. These were going to be notes with terms of five to seven years, and we'd be getting three points of service fees above and beyond what the bank lending to us required. Our repayment schedule with the bank tracked with the anticipated lease payment.

It had the makings of a very nice arrangement, and all we needed to do was replicate this agreement with every piece of leased equipment in New England, cornering this rarely thought of market, and make a killing in the process. It turned out the only thing that would be killed was Best Lease when once again the RTC was involved in stymieing our operation.

To add to the confusion, my chief financial officer told me that he had discovered a problem with the bank applying our monthly note payments. The bank notes had been sent randomly to one of five bank branches, but the bank could not produce the records for where they were posting the payments. We estimated that the amount of money suddenly in limbo between these bank branches totaled about $700,000.

Another bad mail day struck, and we found ourselves the recipients of a terse letter from the bank demanding payment in full on our obligations and a notification that any and all lending to Best Lease was to cease immediately.

Although Best Lease had its wings clipped before it could really fly, this was the beginning of the story about how we had to unwind the relatively few commitments we had made with this bank, which strangely refused to produce the records of the debt I requested after receiving their demand for payment. We were scratching our heads over inconsistencies and missing data, and they weren't giving us anything backing up their figures.

Next, the bank chairmen summoned me to a meeting at their home office. This situation was already heading in a very contentious direction, and the prospect of another court battle loomed, so I went ahead and lawyered up, as it's popular to say now, paying a $10,000 retainer for legal representation that would start at this meeting.

My take was that this bank was reneging on their promises and was not within their rights to call the loan so quickly. And at this point it should be a given that paying up $700,000 was not a possibility. A lot of these businesses and transactions only function because of financed money, and if I had that kind of cash on hand, I probably would've conducted my life in a much different way to begin with.

So going into this meeting, I was fully aware that simply paying up was not an option. As was typical, I knew the chairman and some of the other representatives of the bank, and everything started off cordially with handshakes and smiles. We sat down, and from the very first statement things started to go off the rails.

The bank chairman leaned forward and looked me in the eye.

"You do know you owe a $700,000 balance to the bank?" he said as if it were the most obvious thing in the world. I gave him the same look back.

"Well, show me the records you have from your bank branches, and we'll see," I said.

That didn't really get through to him.

"You do plan to pay it, don't you?" he asked with a nod, fully expecting me to just say yes and dump the money on the table right then and there.

He didn't like it when I said that we'd need to go through the process of reconciling all accounts and records. The local bank lending officer, in charge of our relationship pulled out some ledger papers and passed them over to me, and I saw they were ledger sheets written in pencil with many erased entries allegedly showing which bank branches the note payments had been posted to.

It only took a quick glance to see that these ledger sheets appeared to be inaccurate, and I squinted at them wondering what was actually going on here.

The conversation continued, but like a good song it had a similar refrain. Every few minutes the chairman would chime in with, "Well, Jim, you are going to pay it, right?"

And after a few more choruses of that he added a little something extra that really rankled me.

"You're going to pay this. That's what your reputation says."

My reputation? I thought my reputation was that I didn't lay down for overbearing blowhards from lending institutions making ridiculous unconfirmed demands. This seemed like the exact opposite of that.

"It looks to me like we've got a good ways to go to determine if the balances you claim are authentic, and they need to be backed up by something more meaningful than anything we've seen so far," I said.

I stood up and was ready to walk out, but before I did, I told them that they needed to send us the details so that we could try to match their entries up with ours. We also needed a copy of the ledgers in order to review the postings.

"How do you expect us to know what records we're all working from when you've got five branches involved in this lending process, and nobody seems to know exactly what's owed?"

When the answer I got back was more spineless equivocating, I became extremely suspicious about the chairman, who had almost nothing to say other than trying to get me to admit that I owed the money. It may be glaringly obvious to you after reading this and stacking the clues one on top of another, but for me processing the thought that the bank may not actually have the proper documentation regarding this loan was a revelation.

Imagine being in a fancy boardroom with a bunch of bankers in nice suits who'd been doing this their entire lives, everyone screaming that this was a competently run financial institution, and then taking the leap of faith that it took to seriously consider that these guys actually had no idea how much I really owed them. And all the chairman was doing, like a police interrogation where the officer had to try to bluff the suspect into admitting to the crime when they had no evidence, was to hound over and over again that I needed to confirm that I owed them the money.

And at the same time, it wasn't lost on me that my attorney was as tight-lipped and impassive as a statue in an art museum, which really started to grate on me as well. He didn't say anything the entire time!

The meeting ended, and I walked back with the attorney to his law office. On the way, I had to take the initiative and bring up the topic of the meeting that just ended and the disagreement with the loan, as if such a thing to discuss would've never naturally occurred to this lawyer on his own. Perhaps I would've been better off letting the walk go in silence, because asking him his opinion produced this gem of wisdom.

"You're probably going to have to pay it," he said.

I told him I wanted my $10,000 retainer back, because he was useless. I reminded him that he sat through that entire meeting and apparently hadn't managed to absorb any of what was going on, readily accepting the bank's unsupported position to boot. I don't know what the deal was with this lawyer, but the lights were not on upstairs, that was for sure.

If you like reading about my exploits with bankers, you'll love my forthcoming sequel about all the problems I've had with lawyers. Consider this a teaser.

With that meeting and my former legal representation now firmly in the rearview mirror, the next act in this circus was when the bank sent their commercial lending officer to our offices to discuss payment. I wasn't exactly sure what the point was—if I wasn't going to be paying them sitting in their office, it wasn't going to change things having the same conversation while sitting in mine.

I refused to attend that meeting altogether, telling him in passing that I wouldn't be discussing anything until he produced documents substantiating the basis for his demands. He somehow didn't seem to have anything with him to that effect, and pointing this fact out created a response that one might normally associate with children. He got angry, his face reddening and his voice rising.

Back to our police interrogation analogy: you only have to watch a couple of cop shows to know that when someone lies or bluffs unsuccessfully, they don't then go on to start telling the truth. No, they just lie or bluff in a louder and angrier fashion. That's what was happening here. Their verbal tirades were coming off as desperate and revealed that I actually had the upper hand.

Despite not having any legal counsel to help me arrive at this conclusion, I decided to press forward with a test of my theory.

I told the local branch manager that I wouldn't be making any more payments, because the bank didn't know where the payments were going or how much was owed. This dispute had ended up in a stalemate, so might as well freeze the whole thing.

I expected something to happen. More calls, more demands, more mail. I figured I'd get served and I'd take the same questions I had all along to court in front of a judge, and this time I'd need to get a better lawyer to help me. But on this count, it turned out I was wrong.

Nothing happened…for years. After a while that feeling of waiting for the other shoe to drop turned into that feeling of getting away with something. Then that feeling faded away, the days kept following one another, and to be honest I kind of forgot about the whole issue entirely as other things took up my attention. But that's not the end of the story.

After a few years had passed, I got a call from a large Marina owner who recalled a conversation we'd had when this dispute was going on and had some new information that was going to shed some light on what had happened during this cold case.

Would you believe me if I said this involved another boat? My friend here happened to own a successful marina and had recently sold a boat to the chairman of this bank, and in the process of that found out that while I'd been working on Best Lease the bank had decided to bring all their bank branch's notes, loans, records, and other documents to their home office in Manchester.

My friend remembered our conversation when the dispute was taking place, and he was able to pierce the vale a bit and find out what was happening on the bank's end. It turned out they took all the records of our note from the five branches and loaded them up on a truck to the home office…but they never made it.

Apparently, and I don't blame you if you don't believe this, the bank mixed up the truck carrying the loan records with the truck that they usually send to the dump where old records and papers get destroyed and deposited in the city landfill. To say that again, the bank, acting under their own authority, carried out every last sheet of paper relating to our loans and sent them in a truck to the dump, where they were incinerated and buried underground as ash.

According to what my friend said, the old files meant for the dump were instead loaded onto a different truck and arrived successfully in Manchester at the home office, while all of their records were going up in smoke, including ours.

It's staggering to contemplate how this could've happened or what this really means. Were the two trucks right next to each other, being loaded at the exact same time, and did all the boxes of papers look exactly the same? Think about how many thousands of people were continuing to pay down loans over years or decades, mortgages or anything, when the bank didn't have so much as a sticky-note confirming how much was owed.

That could've been us, and it probably would've been if the bank hadn't initiated an attempt to shut us down. We would've kept paying and paying over for five to seven years until the amount got down to zero.

Instead, that was $700,000 we did not have to pay as our cash flow income crashed as businesses that we held leases for were put out of business unnecessarily, and it was never contested again. Obviously without a funding source, we had to terminate any new activity for Best Lease and slowly discontinue the business, but I'll tell you that at least on one commercial-grade German printing machine we made a pretty penny.

At this point you may be seeing a common denominator in some of these stories in that the operation of these banks was not exactly sterling, and this next one is no different. What is different here is that in this case I let my heart get ahead of my head on a decision I made, which was unusual for me and even rarer after this particular experience.

It all started when one of our banks started getting very aggressive about soliciting us for new loans, making promises on good rates, fast closings, etc. I'd worked with the bank for a long time and didn't expect any trouble from them. And I was right…kind of.

I decided to take them up on their offer for a couple of things, one being financing a nice new office in a 100,000 sq./ft. former manufacturing facility that we purchased and renovated into office condominiums. We kept 12,000 sq./ft. for our upscale offices.

We renovated our offices beyond lovely, the kind of space that made you really want to come in to work, and it had been designed by one of the architects behind Quincy Market in Boston, probably one of the most inviting urban areas in the country that was way ahead of its time. The experience and expertise showed, and this was a decision I'd make again in a heartbeat.

As a plus, the mortgage on that was performing with no issue.

While the office space was undoubtedly a good decision based on sound judgment, the other loan I took out had something else behind it entirely. I decided to make an acquisition of the oldest independent insurance agency in the country, the Mason Insurance Agency, which happened to be located just a few blocks away from our location. Founded in 1837 and by all appearances still going strong, on paper it had the makings of a good purchase that would fit in well with our core business, but I had something else driving me rather than a dispassionate and thorough exercise in due diligence.

Mason Insurance Agency had a storied history having been established in 1837 but I was much more aware of my personal history with it. You see, this was the area's largest insurance agency where I had been recruited to form a partnership to provide Life, Group and formal retirement sales earlier in my career. I have always looked back on my time at Mason with a mix of simmering anger and regret. This was largely the result of the experience I had with the agency owner, a hypocritical city leader that did not live up to his agreement to me, failing to treat me with a bare minimum of respect. When something like that happens, there's only one thing to do. I quit the job.

Leaving the agency on my terms to show that this agency owner had crossed the line and disrespected me and lied about the status of employment agreement terms that he and I had agreed to in a personal meeting with the agency attorney should have been enough, but I wanted more and said something in the heat of the moment that I hadn't forgotten.

As I walked out the door, raising my voice so all could hear, I told him that someday I'd own Mason, the kind of boast that might've seemed foolhardy and laughable at the time, easily brushed off and hopefully forgotten. I mean, people working for a company, quitting, and then coming back to buy the company is just not common. I try to defy expectations though and back up my word whenever possible, and in this unlikely circumstance I actually had the means to follow through on it.

Favorable loan terms actually helped as I was able to combine Mason with my agency. What really made this acquisition possible was the RTC, which had given me a few knocks. They were facing a shrinking business—red flags that I stupidly ignored. I paid $50,000 for an option to two unscrupulous business operators and took great delight in informing the principal owner that I was buying the agency. I let my thirst for come-uppance push me into it. My most notable "emotional" business decision!

OK, it wasn't just a desire for revenge that pushed me into acquiring Mason. When I was working there, the Mason Insurance Agency was a very formidable company with a deep client base that others would've envied. I knew the agency had a sizable position in the local market, and could use the leverage of my agency to get Mason back into a successful position.

That was the idea anyway. The combination of using some of our reserves, negotiating a favorable note with the bank, and using the reserves that Mason had accumulated made this transaction possible.

As we consolidated Mason with my agency, it became clear that many of their customers were original, or so it seemed, from when they started in 1837 and were dying off rapidly. Also, a number of marginal business accounts that they insured were adversely affected by the RTCs negative impact on the NH banks.

We had a significant banking relationship with this bank based on their courting of our divisions, but at a meeting our CFO recommended that we tie down the notes and verify the balances that we owed, as we were generally in default due to the bank's actions foisted upon them by the RTC. Along the way at some point, I sent my CFO over to the bank to get some records about our notes. We wanted to see exactly what the bank was doing with our note balances and for our accounting records, and it never hurt to make sure that everything was lining up and properly documented, as we've seen. And this was before the age of online banking, when a few clicks on a computer could get you access to your records.

Well, it turned out we got a little more from the bank than we bargained for. Yes, the bank was properly documenting everything related to our loans, but that wasn't all. Tucked into the file was the bank's record of all our notes and our payment performance, including some details they no doubt had unintentionally given us.

My CFO came to me and showed me the files, and there it was, plain as day. The bank had written off the Mason and our office notes, meaning that they had each listed with no balance owed so that when payments came in, they were classified as profit. This was something we'd seen before, and it was a relatively common practice, again allowing banks to work the books and present a better picture than there really was.

The total on the two notes came to $1.4 million, consisting of $800,000 for the business and the rest for the balance of Mason Insurance. The notes were consolidated, and that ended up posing a significant cash flow problem for my agency. Suddenly the great terms I'd been promised weren't that great, and with Mason pulling in modest commissions, the situation grew uncomfortable.

The knowledge we gained that the bank had written down the loans to zero after accidentally handing that information to my CFO wasn't of much use until we got to a point where we absolutely had to renegotiate the note. Now that we knew the bank's financial strategy, we were able to devise a plan to capitalize on it.

My plan was to bring a discounted offer to pay off the notes. The bank's focus was quarterly profit to show so-called favorable performance and to generate bonuses for the fair-haired senior officers. By the last two weeks of the quarter, the bank's strategy seems to have been to get whatever they could to apply to overdue notes, allowing them to show a considerable profit provided they accepted quickly. They'd then have a rosier than expected outlook for shareholders, and all the while I'd have the notes paid off with much less than I'd taken them out for. Big "profit" for them, and big real profit, real cash flow savings for us. This is part of the reason I never wanted to get into banking.

All we had to do was dangle the bait and hope that the bank would bite. As one example, my son and I went to the bank at the predetermined time, early the third week of the last month of the quarter when they'd have just enough time to be able to squeak something in and have it appear on their quarterly reports as profit. This wasn't just an attempt to beg for mercy though, and I had an extra trick up my sleeves, something I particularly wanted my son to witness.

When we met with the bank president, I shook his hand and then reached into my pocket for something to give him. What I came up with was an extra set of keys to our office building, and I smoothly deposited them in his hand like he was a valet and I was flipping him the keys to my car. The bank president looked at me in confusion. He wasn't a valet, had probably never been a valet, and had no clue what I was doing.

He asked me what I was doing.

I told him that he could foreclose on the office building, auction it off, and apply the proceeds to what I owed on the building and Mason. That was all I could do cooperatively, and we were going to be out of there within thirty days. I said this was his notice that we were vacating the property within thirty days, because the cash carry on the note was now leaving us underwater, and we'd be better off handing it over to him and running for the exits to relocate.

Now did I really want to leave my beautiful office? No, but he didn't know that. I'd given him the impression that we were one foot out the door with everything we had boxed up and ready to go (and not on a truck to the dump either). I had no intention of leaving but had to play hardball in an attempt to put him in a situation where he had to make a sacrifice to get out of it. After all the bluffing they did, it was my turn to bluff, and the way I sold it was but being firm but relaxed.

When it dawned on him what an auction would actually look like for him, the blood seemed to drain from his face.

"But in foreclosure we wouldn't get twenty-five cents on the dollar!" He was reeling, now looking like he was going to be ill.

"Sorry about that, but it's not my problem," I said, making it seem like I was ready to leave it at that.

At this point it became apparent who was the better bluffer. Maybe I should have gone into playing cards for a living. I'd definitely have done that long before taking a job at a bank.

We did end up leaving him facing the prospect of foreclosure and auction, and the inability of the bank to get anything out of me due to the Irrevocable Trust followed by the IRS lien, letting it really sink in over the next few days so that the bank president could spread the terrible news around his office and get everyone in a mournful mood. Meanwhile, we were busy making arrangements with an insurance company finance arm to advance some money to pay off the note for the building and Mason Insurance.

All we had to do now was come up with something a little less bad for them than what they'd see in foreclosure. On a $1.4 million debt, a quarter on the dollar would've been $350,000, which wasn't that tough to surpass, especially when it meant getting forgiven all the rest of it up to the total amount.

Now that we had something in our pockets to offer, I let my son Chris take on the role of George Clooney in this scheme and head over to visit the bank president solo. I had full confidence that he could get the job done, now that the bank was left in the lurch with everyone in a sour, despondent mood.

My son asked the bank president what it would take to get rid of our loans, and it was unmistakably apparent that they were hungry for cash, and why not? It would all be profit for the quarter on which bonuses would be paid. The negotiations didn't take long, and they ended up landing on the exact number that we'd suspected they would take and that we'd raised from finance: $600,000. That was of course $800,000 less than what was actually owed but a $600,000 cash on notes that had been written off.

My son said that he would be the purchaser but had to clear it with the insurance company lender before making the final commitment, still playing it cool and letting the bank guys continue to sweat it out until it was all signed, sealed, and delivered by the last day of the quarter. But I'm sure that he had a big smile on his face once he was out of sight and getting into his car.

The insurance company lender followed through, as we knew that they would, the paperwork was done, the payment of $800,000 was made to the bank, and we had our copies of the notes marked paid. I've got to tell you that having the $800,000 wiped away was a huge relief, lifting the incredible burden on our cash flow and saving me from the weak performance of Mason Insurance. We went on to organize a separate corporation to own the offices, then integrated Mason Insurance Agency into our agency where we could more easily resuscitate it.

As for the bank, they treated that $800,000 payment like it was mana from heaven, rejoicing in the windfall despite that significantly larger loss that it signified but never disclosed. This was all because they would then be able to turn around and claim a profit to their shareholders. So, they were somehow happy with this arrangement. Now I'm not a financial adviser and this shouldn't be mistaken for investment advice, but maybe this kind of situation is a good reason not to make any investments in banks, especially in adverse economic times!

So, the deal ended up working out OK, and my bacon got saved to a degree by the bank's regrettable (for them) disclosure that they'd already written off the value of the loans. From there, it came down to us recognizing that a little brinkmanship was called for. You have to know when to walk away, and a good time to do that is when the burden of the loan outweighs the value of it.

There are people who get trapped in loans they can't walk away from, particularly when say it's for the house that they live in, but other than that you have to be willing to take the sacrifice and take the loss in order to move on, shifting the burden back to the banks that made the loan.

Considering what these banks have put me through in my life, you might not be surprised to hear that I don't consider these banking obligations sacrosanct, and I'm certainly not going to let a loan drag me down when it's on something that has sunk in value. Prior to the havoc of the RTC takeover of NH banks, I'd never missed a payment or made a late payment on a loan in my life, but at the same time I'm not afraid to take action when the circumstances start to pose a problem. Many people are, allowing themselves to get trapped with obligations that can ruin their lives for years.

Again, it all comes down to the air of authority and respectability that banks try to project. They want you to think that they are invariably trustworthy and working on your behalf to give you the best deal, but over and over again I've seen how they're really just telling their side of the story and expecting you to take them for their word.

This might raise a few eyebrows, but bankers can distort the truth and lie, just like the rest of us can, and that can be true whether it's the bank president to the clerk behind the counter. I'm not saying that there aren't plenty of honest people working at banks, but you've always got to be secure on your position, know your rights and options, and vigorously exercise your prerogative.

chapter seven

Oceanside
Pursuits

While it might seem from the last few chapters that my life fully revolved around insurance and financial issues, there's really a lot more to me than that. In fact, there have been times in my life when I found working in insurance to be a real grind and wanted to distance myself as much as possible. Getting away, enjoying some leisure time, and the calming presence of the ocean have always been important in my life.

But no matter how peaceful the ocean was, frustrating and exasperating situations had a way of tracking me down.

It was back in 1984 when I first decided that the presence of the open sea was something I needed to have in my life. As is often the case, it started with the purchase of a boat, and I wanted to keep it in Kennebunkport, Maine. It was a beautiful area, accessible and friendly, not nearly as renowned and developed as it is now. The place still had the feel of one of those beach towns where you could get away to without being so remote that you wouldn't have access to anything.

The first order of business was checking out the marinas to see where my boat—and I—belonged. It turned out a slip was available at the aptly named Kennebunkport Marina, a privately held operation that seemed to have the kind of clientele I'd fit in with. The slip cost $5,000, and I jumped at it, having my attorney prepare the conveyance and get the transaction completed.

One thing stuck out in my mind during this time that turned out to be somewhat prophetic. Once the deal was done and I now had the means to traverse the ocean to my heart's delight, my lawyer had an offhand parting comment.

"So, you bought a boat and now a slip. What's next?"

I brushed off the comment, thinking it was nothing, but it quickly turned out he was right to think this was leading in a certain direction and the train had not yet reached its destination.

I must've made some kind of impression on the marina owner, because he came to me one day and asked if I wanted to be partners. 50/50, right down the middle. On the one hand, I appreciated the business and the boost it might give me in the area to not just say that I was there with a boat but had half the Kennebunkport Marina as well. But this current owner was a guy that I didn't have a high comfort level with. He had some personal issues that I found unpleasant to a degree.

And now this guy was coming to me asking if I wanted to give him $450,000 for half the marina. I had to weigh the potential of the business with the current owner's idiosyncrasies, and the Magic 8 Ball said yes, I should do it. When I called my attorney to tell him I was taking this next step, he laughed.

That worked out well for about two years, but it wasn't the end of the story. About six months later my partner came to me and told me that we were out of money, which I found unsurprising, especially in view of the fact that I had not been paid one dime! My involvement had been largely passive, seasonal, and social, but the marina was full of boats, so I could only imagine what kind of mismanagement had been going on for the money to run out.

I told him I didn't know what he was talking about, but that I wasn't out of money.

That may have been an offhand comment, but he quickly seized on it.

"Well, you're gonna have to buy me out for the other half."

There weren't two ways about it. Either I was going to have to hand over another $450,000 to take sole possession of the marina, or he'd continue to run it into the ground until it folded up, causing me to lose everything. More than anything, getting rid of this guy was the priority, and I could only imagine how he'd blow my next $450,000 after losing what I'd given him before. The marina was perfect for a "dockominiums" project that, by our estimates, could double our money.

As was my habit of carrying a briefcase with different business contracts, I immediately pulled out a Purchase & Sale Agreement, filled in the space and had him sign after which I gave him a deposit of $10,000 on the spot. But we entered into a purchase and sale agreement for this amount that would make me 100% owner of the marina.

In my mind I was no longer Jim the insurance and real estate guy. I was now Jim the salty Maine marina owner, tying Bowline knots with ease and plucking five-pound lobsters out of the ocean with my bare hand. OK, maybe not, but I did enjoy the idea of it.

Our insurance business at the time was going very strong, leaving me in search of another challenge. The agency and our profit center comprised of partial ownership in sixty-seven small insurance agencies throughout New England, and it was growing at a pace in a way that felt effortless on my part. The guy who was putting in the effort was Nick Pappajohn, who'd been with me for thirty-eight years until I sold my interest, and he was doing a phenomenal job.

That put me on autopilot for a while, allowing me to focus my efforts on my new marina empire in Kennebunkport.

While the previous owner, now fully departed, had been content to let things roll in and out from one day to next like the tide, I was a little more industrious than that and had a mind to innovate and grow. Here's where the story gets interesting.

I began to integrate some of the techniques and methods I had going for my other businesses into the marina game. I owned a development project, which was cut up into what were called pods, grouping different forms of housing including condominiums.

But now, I needed a home in the Kennebunkport area, but I did not have the cash to buy one. At the time we had a very large condo project under construction that was doing very well. There was one developer in New Hampshire who was very interested in the project and came to me with a proposition that would allow him to buy roughly thirty units. I smelled a tax-free exchange under the new IRS regulations.

My position was that I didn't want the cash and instead preferred to trade on the value for a home in the Kennebunk Beach area abutting Kennebunkport, which would allow me to be there more. He agreed, and I found a home that appraised for $291,000, and this was just about the same as what I'd charged the developer for the lots, so it was an even deal. I was excited about my new place on the Atlantic Ocean that came at no cost, but as was often the case, I had a few ideas for what to do with it.

Alright, it wasn't exactly at no cost. The next tax season rolled around, and my CPA let me know the IRS didn't allow tax-free exchanges on residential property. They expected me to hand $50,000 over to them for it, and did I mention this conversation took place on April 15th? That turned out to be a busy day, but we got it done, and that was my cost basis for a home overlooking the ocean.

My grand innovation for the marina business was to create the first "dockominium marina" project in the northeast, which happened to be the very first one along the entirety of the Atlantic Ocean. We changed the name of the marina to the Kennebunkport Yacht Club and placed all of the docks in separate ownership that could be sold individually to boaters. They were not cheap yet sold quickly, and the project was highly successful. My old marina partner no doubt sorely regretted shaking me down too soon and missing out on all of this extra money he could've blown.

So, at this point I had a thriving marina club, a waterfront home, and of course a boat. Enough? Not quite.

I was actually just getting on a roll, and now that I firmly had my foot in the door it seemed like I couldn't turn around without bumping into another incredible opportunity that I couldn't pass up. It seemed like everybody running a business was looking for an exit, though I'm sure they regretted it once the massive growth in the area started to become apparent.

The owner of a large motel in Kennebunkport was ready to walk away, and he'd heard I was making some investments in the area. That was another deal in the books for a very successful operation, particularly in the summer months when the tourists came to town. Now I had a place for any friends I wanted to drag out to the oceanside as well.

But there was more to the area than just what other people had put up, and my spending spree continued with several vacant lots in a new development that a contractor was going to help me put homes on.

I was on a real roll and felt like I was taking over the town, getting established as a primary mover and shaker. However, I kept a very low presence, refusing to join the most prominent social and boating club in Kennebunkport after my local attorney pushed me to do so.

The Kennebunkport Yacht Club was doing fantastically with our new business model, and it got the attention of the owner of the marina next door, which was called Chicks Marina. This place had a somewhat different approach, serving as a transient boat facility that was also the largest dealer for Boston whaler boats, Mako boats, Yamaha engines, and Mercury engines. So, this was a whole different ballgame compared to the stuff I'd already been involved with, and now I had two marinas, ninety slips, and quite a long stretch of water frontage.

JIM MASIELLO

If people have heard of Kennebunkport, it's probably because of its most famous residents, the Bush family, who really did a lot to draw attention to this area and make it a coveted stretch of coastline.

President HW Bush 41 was at our Marina a fair amount as we launched his boat (only boat ramp in Kennebunkport). I was usually there when he came to the Marina, and I would always know because we had his Secret Service boats docked there. I would stand on the ramp to make sure the boat was OK, and we would visit. We knew each other pretty well as I was very involved in his Presidential campaign.

I can remember the night he had surprisingly beaten Ronald Reagan in the Iowa primary and flew directly to Keene to begin a statewide campaign swing that I had worked on. I picked him up at the airport, took him to my home so he could rest and get cleaned up for his swing, and then off we went early the next morning. I vividly remember when he was getting dressed that night. We were talking and he said, "Jimmy, watch how I put my slacks on." He proceeded to do so and said, "Always remember, one leg at a time." And that summed up his philosophy!

He loved his boat and was on it a fair amount. Fishing was his love. My younger son Matt was a very favorite of his as his reputation relative to fishing was apparent. When the helicopters would fly into his home from Portsmouth where Air Force One would land, his first marine radio transmission to my son was always, "Matt, where are the fish biting?" Our boat was the only one allowed inside the security zone around his boat.

I always like to tell the story of one of our real estate managers. She asked me if I would take her husband and sons fishing sometime in our boat. I found the time as I usually did and made a date. Her husband (also a principal of the local junior high school) arrived at the marina and participated in getting the gear and bait ready to go before we set out. He was very unfamiliar with the boat or any boat for that matter.

We left the dock and as we went by 41's home, I told him we may see him fishing. We got our lines and bait into water, and it was not long before we had a nice bluefish on. I left the wheel and the boat in idle while we wrestled the fish into the boat. His son was ecstatic. A short time later, Dad got a bluefish on line. I started getting radio calls from the Associate Press reporter who was out in another boat shadowing Bush 41. He asked if I would take his film in so it could be aired that night on national TV. We were done anyway so I said yes, and we maneuvered to our position and picked his film up. While this was going on, I asked the father to man the radio for any calls. A call did come over, and it was Bush 41 looking for me. I spoke with him and told him where we were and that the blues were biting. About ten minutes later, I could see the Armada coming towards my boat and pulling up next to us. It was the President of the United States. As usual, we had a nice greeting, and he met the sons and father.

I never gave this another thought, as for me this was pretty standard. So we headed to the dock to cook our catch. After we were done with the day, the father said "thank you" to me and went on about how he'd never been on the ocean in a boat, never caught any fish, certainly never met the president. He was clearly overwhelmed with what he'd just experienced.

I happened to be at the marina filling in for my GM when one of our slip owners, a guy who'd generally appear at the marina on Sunday mornings with vodka in hand, said that he and his wife owned an oceanfront home a short distance from President George HW Bush. I knew the house and location. He was always hoping to sell it to me (or anyone else—it was overpriced but right on the Atlantic), and I was open to the prospect of rubbing elbows with the folks over there, but this guy's wife was ill, and I told him I'd only buy it if his wife was agreeable about it.

I went with Bill to speak with his wife, a lovely lady who was battling cancer. It was fine by her, paving the way for our purchase agreement on the house for $750,000. This was a trade up from the Kennebunk Beach after renovations and two years of ownership which I sold at a hefty $600,000 profit, which I used for the new home and paid the rest in cash.

I hired a contractor to check the place out, and what we discovered was almost enough to make him faint. The insulation was all bad and a lot of other aspects of the home were outdated, not done properly, or dangerous.

We ended up tearing the entire house down with direct views and access, leaving only the fireplace and chimney. Then with our project architect we started nearly from scratch, putting together plans for a stunning 7,000 sq./ft. home with all windows facing the ocean. I even had a saltwater pool built on the rocks bordering the ocean.

The estimate from my construction company to build the home was around $500,000. Retail would have been around $700,000. So, I secured a jumbo mortgage for the $500,000 amount and was looking forward to having a beautiful home in Kennebunkport on the point next to the Bush compound.

Unfortunately, there were rough seas and stormy weather ahead, and with my other financial responsibilities, as has been documented in other chapters, it was becoming apparent that this was all becoming too much to manage and my dreams of stepping into the role of being a dominant presence in Kennebunkport were heading out to sea.

Prior to my financial calamity, I had that appraisal on the property for $1.5 million, and I used that as the basis for an ad in the Wall Street Journal pitching the new home for sale. Some time passed, there weren't any bites, and the pressure to liquidate some of these assets grew and grew. I lowered the price listed in the ad gradually, and after about six months I finally got a call from a serious buyer.

As we talked, I got a weird impression that the voice sounded familiar, and I finally had to just stop and ask who was on the other end. The guy turned out to be the owner of a gas and oil company in Massachusetts, and my agency carried his insurance. Although the association was nice, it didn't do wonders for the prospects on this property. His offer was only $750,000, and I was compelled to take it when the alternative was a swift foreclosure and loss.

At least this way I still netted $250,000 on the transaction, funds that were sorely needed and quickly spent. And what I still had when all was said and done was both much more modest than what I'd had and still an extreme luxury that I'd never stopped appreciating. I did not have the home in Kennebunkport anymore. For about a year, I had no home and was living out of a model home in one of our developments—quite a comedown.

It was at this point that I sold Chick's Marina to the buyer who had been constantly on me to do so. I paid $2.2 million for it three years prior, but that included the boat and motor inventory. The buyer was notorious for gobbling up properties and businesses in the area who excelled at promoting his success and materialistic possessions.

I still owed about $1 million to the bank who financed my purchase. For this transaction to work, the buyer needed a one-year co-signor on the note he was financing. I got the bank paid off, and they relegated my debt to no balance due conditioned on my agreeing to co-sign, so I did. That relieved me of another $1 million in debt. I also had floor plan financing for the inventory and that was conveyed to the buyer.

The negotiation started with a bang. The buyer was noted for his negotiation skills. We used my office, and I had my CFO as did the buyer have his. I knew what to expect as his reputation preceded him. The first two hours, I listened to him listing and telling me everything wrong with the marina and his estimated cost to fix it.

As noon was growing closer, I said we were going to break for lunch and reconvene at 1 p.m. He objected and wanted to continue. My response was that I was unaware of the many issues with my marina, and I wanted time to digest them before he made his counteroffer. My CFO and I walked out of the meeting, and I said, "See you at one."

My CFO was very nervous because he knew as well as I that it was VERY important to sell and get rid of the debt. I told him to relax as the buyer wanted the marina badly as he was boasting around town that he was going to own it regardless of the cost. By the way, he was a short guy with a big belly, but in his mind, he was brilliant and highly successful.

We cordially reconvened at 1 p.m. He reintroduced his CFO who was a retired Nun. And there she was negotiating with a former catholic school student who was denied being an altar boy but required to make the sacrament with the nuns.

Now I was ready. I thanked the buyer for bringing all of the deficiencies of the Marina to my attention much to his surprise. I decided to spice up the negotiation and told him that his rhetoric was bullshit. Also, I said, "Screw you. If you want to own this, don't treat us the way you have been acting, like a complete asshole." To spice it up for the nun's presence, I said, "Let's stop playing f____ing games," which sure threw the nun's composure for an obvious loop.

I said, "You know we have not discussed price during the three hours of discussion. My price is $2.6 million and further negotiation is NOT necessary." I got up to walk out when he said, "Wait, you won't consider a counteroffer?" I said, "Absolutely not! Why would you want to own such a shit hole?" He agreed to the $2.6 million and we had our attorneys draw the papers. That further reduced my bank debt by another $1 million.

When I bought Chick's Marina, it was subject to an inventory. It was run so poorly, I took a chance that we could find something to effectively reduce the price. Interestingly, we were short one boat and an engine. I could have called the deal off, but Chicks' head technician let slip that the owner had given the Whaler Sales manager both for free. That clearly was a conflict. Although we were the largest whaler dealer, we still had way too much inventory.

So, I set a "get to meet" meeting up with the Whaler sales manager. After some small talk, I gave him a report that showed, based on sales history, that Whaler had been dumping way too many boats on us. I asked him if they could take some back to redistribute to other dealers. He responded, "No, that is not part of our franchise agreement." So I said, "OK, but can you return your boat and motor that you did not pay for?" He stiffened up. I then told him we could do this the easy way and he could keep the boat and motor, or I would have this conversation with the Whaler CEO with whom I had a meeting scheduled. We were able to significantly reduce our inventory as truck haulers began taking the overstock back to Whaler or to other dealers. This was a great help in reducing our floor plan debt.

After the Chick's sale, I had to deal with Kennebunkport Yacht Club and the remaining slips that were for sale. I just wanted the debt to be gone. I estimated the remaining value to be over $800,000. I met with the bank and said, "If I can get you around $500,000, would you agree to let me sell it and forgive the balance?" They agreed so I called one of the slip owners and offered the deal. He was a former banker and a damn good one. Bottom line, he said, "Let's do it!" I made the arrangements with the bank and pocketed around $300,000, and another $800,000 of debt disappeared.

The Yacht Club docks became successful as soon as docks opened for sale. The largest and most expensive dock went early. Living in the area was a hedge fund investor who had just acquired the largest US men's underwear company in the US. His offices were in the Sears Building in Chicago. I met with him for this discussion. He was about 5'6", and cocky could not even start to describe him and his captain, who would be living on the boat.

We consummated the deal and he put a 63' Magnum boat in the slip. There were only three of these boats ever made. Two were in the Med and the third one in Kennebunkport.

The cocky guy was very successful, and he let it be known. One day two middle-aged women came to meet with me (former nuns) and said that the owner wanted to sell me back the dock and named a crazy price. I said no thanks.

About a month or so passed when I got served with a Federal Court warrant to appear at a hearing in a Federal Court. I was being sued for a number of things. Well, we went to court and listened to the charges against me all with the result of legally requiring me to purchase the dock for a greatly exacerbated price.

Something about this whole process smelled. The boat was no longer in the slip. The rumor was that the owner had bought a 200' luxury boat that he docked off his house nearby. It occurred to me that he was up to something, so I bought a "Yachting" magazine that lists expensive boats for sale. Guess what, a nice ad for a 63' Magnum (only three were made) was occupying a nice half-page ad. Simply stated, the owner bought a much bigger boat and was trying to sell the slip because he had no need for it. So, he was suing to compel me to pay him $500,000 for his dock when he paid around $200,000.

The judge had this figured out. Here we go again, only this time it was a lawyer from Chicago and one from Boston who wanted to meet with me before the trial began. I raised their ire when I said I don't meet on the courthouse steps.

Our attorney presented our case and the Yachting Magazine ad which clearly pointed up the reason for the suit. It was dismissed in about a one-hour session by the judge.

When we were walking out, one of the attorneys said, "You know we can work this out." I looked him right in the eye and guess what my response was? **Screw you.**

chapter eight

Stop the Bleeding

On this journey through my professional, political, and personal lives, we've seen situations where I've won big and some where I scraped by. Banks have been a common feature in these stories, and their behavior has been at times predatory or incompetent or both. But I've also seen them groveling and desperate to the point where I might actually have some sympathy for them.

Like any other kind of business, banks are liable for the decisions they make and the twists of fate that determine the outcome of the loans they get involved with. Even if they have the upper hand, they become subject to the people who come to them for loans. It's not a one-way street, and even the most thorough vetting can allow a deal to get through that can cripple the bank.

I'd like to tell you about the Eastfield project, one that I became tangentially involved with and mostly watched from a distance like a head-on collision that you pass while driving down the road. It was just impossible to look away.

One day, I got a call from the president of one of our attentive banks, a guy who was a good friend and had always done right by us. He wanted me to drop by his office, and I told him I was more than happy to do so. The subject of the meeting wasn't even obliquely referenced, but I didn't think much of it at the time. After all, this was the same banker/friend who picked me up at my office unannounced to go to his home (my former home) to show me the new gas grill that he had just bought. When we got there, we went to the grill, and he started telling about all of its great new features. Then he said, "Watch how easy it lights." That was when I stepped back, and sure enough when he fired it up there was a minor explosion singing his eyebrows and messing his suit up.

When I got there, I was surprised to find out that this bank president was hoping to talk to me about a development project we'd already reviewed at their behest and turned down. I was already a bit astonished. It was one thing for a bank to present an offer, but having them come back to me hat in hand about this was something I hadn't expected, and it couldn't have been easy for him.

He told me all about the Eastfield project, the loan he had out on a piece of land in a remote section by a not-so-nice small town outside the city. His greatest concern was that the builder on the project did not have much experience, resulting in costly overages that were putting the loan near default. We were both looking at a slow-motion crash in progress, and he wanted to know if there was anything that could be done to avert the worst-case scenario.

For my part, I didn't hesitate to offer some free advice from the comfort of my chair with the whole thing at arm's length. I advised him that the absolute last thing he'd want to do was make it known that the project might be foreclosed upon, as that would lower the value of the whole thing.

But the bank president hadn't just called me in for a few pointers, and he asked if I'd be willing to take over the project on very favorable terms.

The unfortunate thing for him was that even favorable terms would not be enough to overcome the extremely unfavorable aspects of this project.

I went through all the reasons I'd turned down the project in the first place. Not only was the town not attractive, but that particular location was an eyesore as well, something no amount of construction could fix. Some areas were just in vogue, others just comfortably moving along, but this area had a negative reputation and a lack of popularity that had the market moving at a snail's pace. Nobody wanted to be there, least of all me.

As much as I hated to issue another rejection to a guy I knew who was looking for help, I had to evaluate the project on the merits, and the long and the short of it was it didn't make sense for me when the buildout would be so slow and the tenuous margins at risk. These were all things I'd told them before, and instead of listening to me the bank chose to enter the project with someone else instead of walking away.

The glum look on the guy's face as he said that the bank was stuck with it said it all. We were having a "told you so" moment, and the circumstances this bank was facing were dire.

With no way out, the bank was forced to continue moving forward while hoping for the best. The builder started to construct homes on speculation, which only increased the balance on the bank loan. Despite what appeared to be progress, things were still not going well, and I got another call from the president with a request to assess what was going on with the project.

After looking through the new numbers and the growing amount of red ink, it was apparent to me that continuing with the project was only digging themselves deeper, when what they had to do was get out as soon as possible by whatever means necessary. I told him to stop the bleeding, but he was still looking at me as a way to rescue the project. I can't blame him for wanting to find an alternative to losing everything they'd put in, but we were doing well and had no reason to take a risk with that amount of debt even if the terms were incredibly favorable, as they were offering.

My team and I did end up discussing the offer, and we felt like there was something we could do to help, but the only way it would work was if the bank would accept terms they'd scarcely ever contemplate otherwise. I told the president we'd have to do two things in order to get involved: accept no liability—zero—for the debt and increase the loan in order to facilitate additional work on the project.

The prospect of completely handing over a project to us while still retaining all liability was a tough pill to swallow, but the bank was stuck between a rock and a hard place, and I was somehow the only one in position to help. He accepted a deal with terms that other bankers would've cried or laughed about depending on their sensibilities.

So, we were now stepping into this project in a unique position where we weren't responsible for anything that we did, and we had plenty of money to do things like construct the road, improve amenities, and put together affordable-sized homes. With the help of our architect, we got to work on a new plan for Eastfield that included some attractive designs but lower square footage, and we decided to only build homes as they were sold. The bank would get 100% of the net profit.

This allowed us to continue working without digging the bank deeper, and if it turned out we got stuck we could simply walk away from the whole thing. I told the bank president myself that he got himself into this mess after we had turned it down. He hadn't listened when I told him it was a bad site, and that it would not be a viable location for timely success. The message didn't get through to him then, but he heard me loud and clear now that it was too late.

Over the course of the next year, we actually did manage to build a few houses, sell them, and start paying down the bank loan. This was hardly turning into a win though, merely just a way for us to tread water, and our ability to continue to do that was coming to an end.

One day I went in to meet with the bank president to deliver the news that the project was diverting too much of our attention from other viable projects. We couldn't afford to keep plugging away at this, but we had made substantial progress and had turned a colossal mess into an active project.

As with many of our other conversations, he wasn't pleased with the result of this one, but he'd known what kind of situation we were entering into at the start. Although some of the lots sold with new homes, there was much left undone and now no one the bank could get to work on it. I don't know how much they lost through the foreclosure process, but it had to be around $2 million.

My gut feeling about the property and the thoroughly investigated investment had both clued me in that this was a loser, and being right in this circumstance had saved me from taking such a big loss myself. I told the bank president that in the future I'd be happy to vet any project that seemed viable, going through all the motions with a marketing plan and everything, but we weren't a charity, and the bank wasn't a charity case.

I paid for lunch and walked away from Eastfield, though some of our expenses were carried on our books and needed to be written off. Sometimes when you bend over backward to help someone, you still end up knocking your head if you lean too far. Once again though, it served as a sterling lesson in how banking wasn't the right field for me and never would be.

chapter nine

The Dairy Farm

As you can tell, I've been fortunate enough in my career to gain experience in a wide variety of areas and industries. Complex, difficult situations were bound to arise no matter what sector of the economy we were dealing with, and the thing that always made it worthwhile to me were the people involved. Relationships, respect, and loyalty are everything and have made me who I am, but not everyone attempts to live by those principles as much as I have.

There was a very successful dairy farm operation in the area, which had been run by a man with something of an infamous reputation up until his death, at which time the farm passed to his two sons.

In addition to the farm, the father had seemingly passed down something of his acrimonious nature to his sons, who had a very nasty relationship with one another. This farm had been a real institution in the area, but this abrupt transition was threatening to ruin everything.

I got a call from the older brother who was a friend with a request to meet as soon as possible. He wanted to discuss the future of the farm, which was now jointly owned by the two brothers, and how best to manage a tense situation between them. Wouldn't you know, the younger brother called me as well with the same request. And to top it all off these two brothers lived together with their families in a large, beautiful, old farmhouse sealed off and split into two distinct units; they were still basically living together with only a wall between them.

The potential sources of tension were everywhere, and I learned more as I talked to them and heard about what was going on. While the relationship between the brothers was extremely volatile, and both of them were equally hardheaded, in my experience there's always one person who's really driving the conflict. In this situation, it seemed to be that it was actually the older brother's wife who was responsible for probably seventy-five percent of the strife.

In typical farm style, I would have to meet separately at 5:30 a.m. in the barn with each brother to discuss the situation while they were handling milking duties. I did my best to keep everyone calm and level-headed, but it seemed like the conversation and topic of what would happen to the farm was a minefield where any innocuous comment could set someone off.

They wanted my recommendation on how to split their inheritance so that they could completely separate without any common ground or interests yet they both enjoyed and only knew dairy farming. That seemed best, since they genuinely disliked each other and weren't going to be able to work together. At the same time, just splitting up the farm wasn't going to be an easy feat.

I couldn't just tell them each to take half the cows and go their respective ways. It looked like another challenging situation, but I believed there was an opportunity here to make everybody happy as long as the relationships didn't spiral out of control into sabotage.

They wanted to move on from each other, but the strained relationship made it difficult to hear anything that wasn't immediately to their liking. I

SCREW U

ended up calling them both blockheads to their face over the course of the conversation when they would close their minds just as I started bringing up an idea.

I told them I was going to have to move forward with an idea on my own without even sharing what it was with either of them. Since I had a lot of other projects going on, that was going to have to be done on my schedule, and they had to take my word for it that it would be fair. Their respective attorneys did get an overview, but that was it, and the brothers basically left me to my devices.

After all, they knew me well enough to both call me. The least they could do was give me a chance to sort it all out without them shooting it down in a knee-jerk fashion out of spite for each other.

As with pretty much all real estate deals and transactions, the very first step was to review a city tax map that had all the pertinent details about the farm property, the boundaries, assessment, zoning use status, etc. Once we had that and understood that we were dealing with a relatively expansive property, my plan really started to take shape.

There was going to be a way to divide the property in two that ultimately provided roughly equal value to both brothers, even if one side retained all the dairy farm business and assets. This other half of the property consisted of fields and maple trees that were used to produce and sell maple syrup, but that was far from the highest and best use for that area. The trick was that this section had absolutely no infrastructure—roads, water, utilities, etc.—which meant that it was an uphill battle to create value in that area with a development.

We moved forward with a plan to add the necessary infrastructure and plan a building lot development that would comply with local planning and zoning restrictions and have a likely chance of success with planning board approval. The brothers pretty much only spoke to me, never each other, and there was always a danger that one of them would pull the plug.

Another lynchpin of the deal was that the older brother wanted to continue with the existing dairy farm while the younger brother didn't want anything to do with him, meaning there wasn't any fighting over that part of it. But we did have to do a lot of work to show the younger brother that the bare fields and trees were worth as much as the thriving family dairy business.

We called the newly subdivided area "The Meadows" and planned condominiums in a very low-density plan (our development division trademark), a relatively smaller unit count than might otherwise be allowed due to more favorable zoning rules, but it was going to be enough to get us where we needed to go. We needed to find a buyer for the development. Conceptually, the plan was focused on when it got built out, and when the lots were sold the younger brother would be paid off for his half and be free to leave, allowing the older brother to stay on his half with the farm to continue to work it sans any interference.

The last part of the puzzle was that neither brother believed in borrowing nor putting the dairy farm in debt to accomplish any of this. It was all going to have to be self-financed on the basis of the subdivision pro forma with an expectation of a certain profit margin after setting net prices after development expenses on each condo lot.

More and more the situation looked like a typical development once many of these details with the brothers and their exit were sorted out. I stood to gain from assembling the subdivision plan, the development, and from any real estate transaction dealings that took place.

While both the brothers had been sincere, bordering on desperation in their inquiries to me, I'd always had a sneaking suspicion that something would go wrong, but the outlook became more favorable all the time. I continued to meet with the brothers—separately, of course—and their enthusiasm for the plan only grew. Each was going to be getting what they wanted financially, with the added bonus of being able to get rid of each other while continuing to be dairy farmers.

The closing approached with everything seeming like it was going to be wrapped up neatly, but as the saying goes, nothing is over until it's over. All these brothers had to do was be in a room together with their respective lawyers to go over some documents and provide signatures for fifteen minutes max, and then it would all be done, the strategic plan in place and everyone could move on.

What do you think? If you stood to gain a huge amount from an inheritance, and all you had to do to get it was be in a room with a family member you disliked for a short period of time, could you do it without ruining everything? These brothers couldn't, or maybe I should say more precisely that these families couldn't.

Closing day came, and there was no reason for me to attend. My work was done except for finding a buyer to develop the younger brother's acreage and approved subdivision. Our focus was implementing building the project, and all these brothers needed to do was get together with their attorneys to execute the agreements. I figured if worse came to worse the attorneys would be able to manage keeping everyone in line, but instead the best the attorneys could do was place a frantic phone call to me.

"Can you come over to this closing right now?" he begged, the fear of God in his voice.

Of course, I had no choice but to drop everything and rush over as fast as I could before it all fell apart. When I got there, I discovered that the older brother's wife hadn't been able to keep herself from stirring the pot and trying to seize a little more.

I had to say that I wasn't going to be able to get involved if the wives were in the room. It was going to be hard enough to get the two brothers to settle this. Having to deal with all four was an impossible task to juggle when everyone wanted to come out on top and feel like they were getting the better end of it. Wasn't inheriting a successful dairy farm free and clear enough?

After I asked the wives to leave the meeting, I asked them what this was about, and the older brother said he didn't think the younger brother should be getting all the income from the maple trees on the Meadows subdivision side. My jaw dropped open.

"This is about the maple trees?" I gasped.

"Well, it's very important to my wife," he said. Oh boy.

We hammered out a plan for the older brother to tap the trees for the maple syrup for three years, but he had to share in the profits from the maple syrup profits, which mercifully was acceptable to the younger brother, who was really going to be seeing his income coming from the development anyway. By the end of it, a lot of those trees weren't even going to be there.

Now that we'd cleared the air, the papers were signed and the subdivision they'd agreed to was officially created. The next step was finding a buyer for the now-available subdivision, which we laid out in pods so that a builder could take a few of the lots without having to take on the entire subdivision. We wanted to offer maximum flexibility about transferring the lots, but we maintained strict control over the construction design, landscaping plans, and even the color of all the units.

Builders wouldn't be able to add so much as an awning without our say so. We wanted to make sure everything met a specific quality threshold, otherwise the neighborhood property values could be severely skewed if someone came in and wanted to custom-design something weird and unattractive.

As we got farther along in the process, it turned out that the older brother's wife was right to want some of the maple syrup money, because based on surveys and the town tax assessment, the approved Meadows subdivision had an estimated net value that exceeded the value of the remaining family farm. We had an idea to exchange the new Meadows subdivision to the younger brother for complete ownership of his own dairy farm in a way that would be tax free, and that would get us to a place where they were finally even.

At this point our construction and development division went forward with the necessary infrastructure installation to support the new neighborhood, and because of the logistics and site condition this was a very expensive development to create from a utility, design, and engineering standpoint.

One important point that I stressed was that the surveyor and engineer needed to keep one foot of land along the road layout between the new Meadows road and the existing dairy farm now owned by the older brother as a buffer.

I'd been suspicious that the older brother might want to set aside some of the farmland abutting the Meadows for a smaller subdivision, and sure enough before long he caught the development bug and wanted to see if he could build some units of his own to up his profits from the deal. We were not included in this process.

There was just one problem—that one-foot buffer now separated his property from the road and utilities that ran through the area!

When he found out that the Meadows owned a one-foot stretch running along his side of the road, which was going to threaten the subdivision plan he'd submitted that utilized the road and utilities extending from the Meadows, he was not very happy!

He came storming into my office asking me what the hell we did giving away his land like that. Well, it was never his part of the land, and it had been his idea to have the road farther into the other property because he didn't want it running along his property. Whoops!

I can't read anybody's mind or see the future. I was only able to go by what he said, and it seemed like he wanted the development at arm's length so that he could run his dairy farm with as much space as possible, and he dictated his terms in accordance with that. His lack of foresight ended up costing him, probably because he and his wife were more concerned with thinking about the maple trees that were there rather than the possible buildings that weren't there yet.

That probably made for some bitter pancake breakfasts.

This whole process took about a year to finalize. While it was a rocky road at several points and could've fallen through, from our perspective it worked out fine. Our real estate company controlled all development and other aspects of the real estate sales, and guaranteed an exclusive ability to serve as agents.

Deals like that, though perhaps somewhat bittersweet for the older brother, always remind me to keep perspective and remember what you started with. Both brothers got everything they wanted out of the deal, and that was the important thing even if one wasn't able to extract every last possible drop of value out of the land.

As if it wasn't hard enough to get this deal to completion between these two brothers, the story of how this development came to be was far from over, and it was not pretty.

Sure, we'd worked out a plan with these two families about how to handle their inheritance by putting a big development on their land, but as we've seen, actually getting the development there came with the usual struggles. By this point, can you guess who managed to make a mess of it?

The tax-free exchange and the development plan were completed. We were working on approvals and looking ahead to breaking ground. That meant we now needed to get the project financed, allowing us to go ahead and create this neighborhood that we were all so excited about. It was time to get the profits off paper and into our pockets.

This was a difficult idea for the farmer owner trying to sell his farm in a nearby town, who was a bit antiquated in his thinking and found debt and financing unappealing, even if it meant more money in his pocket. Subordinating to a local bank rubbed him the wrong way. The alternative to taking on debt and building out the development ourselves, though, was basically unthinkable. We'd have to sell the vacant lots directly to the residential owners, leaving us with a fraction of what we'd get if we did more ourselves.

The farmer started to get the picture once we explained it all to him in a number of meetings, and what we did was assign values to each lot consisting of the amount he would get when the finished homes on them sold. Again, this was more than he would get if the lots were sold as is.

Also, his income from his farm sale could go up another 25%. Not hard to understand.

We had a local builder who specialized in smaller, quality homes that young families typically used as starters get involved. We grouped lots into "pods," with that builder getting some, many remaining with us, and other pods available for other builders or ourselves if they were still there by the time we were ready to get to them.

All told we were looking at 130 homes in this development with a substantial upside in the millions of dollars. Adding grease to the fire, the housing market was as strong as it had been in years, making it the perfect time to bring all these units forward.

I expected the financing portion of this to be easy and went to my favorite local bank. The guys there salivated over the opportunity to participate in the development. It was an easy sell on our part, and for all the world I thought this was over and done with for all intents and purposes.

Then the bank CEO gave me a call to tell me that he'd worked out a deal with another local bank to co-fund the project. While that shouldn't have affected anything, I had to tell him I didn't have a good relationship with the other bank. Still, it was his decision to make, and I wasn't too worried about our plan, considering how strong it was.

It surprised me that my bank needed another to co-fund the project, limiting their own benefit of participating, but I didn't let it get to me. We signed the deal, got access to the funding, and it should've all been routine from that point on.

As expected, executing the development plan worked out great, better than we'd projected even, thanks to the strong housing market, the good location, and the appeal of our designs. Houses were being built and sold faster than anyone would've anticipated, putting the huge success we'd all envisioned in reach.

We made it all the way to our third renewal of our note with the bank before we got a sudden dousing of cold water. The loan officer wasn't preparing to renew the note with us, an inexplicable move considering that we'd faithfully been paying it down as we were obligated to with each and every home sale.

At that point we had a number of homes under construction, quite a few that were built and ready to close, and then several model homes in place that would eventually become available. This all amounted to a large degree of expended investment capital that was suddenly at risk if the bank pulled the plug on us.

Time for another fabled meeting with our financial partners, and this time two bank presidents were involved.

Once the meeting began, the lead president, the one I'd worked most closely with and favored, told me that the two banks were having a problem agreeing to the previously agreed upon note terms between them and that it had nothing to do with our performance. The second bank wanted the terms of the bank's agreement changed. This was a dispute between the banks through no fault of ours. Apparently, there were other issues between the two banks that did not involve us or our financing terms and performance. I asked if I was here to referee the dispute or discuss our project. I was quick to add that this didn't surprise me considering the incompetency of the other bank president.

I couldn't have been in a better position, and all they had to do was keep agreeing to what they'd already agreed to in order to continue making money. This was an issue for them to resolve themselves, and I was in disbelief that it had gotten to the point where I even had to hear about it. Weren't they supposed to be professionals?

The conversation continued, and I got the sneaking suspicion that what was happening in front of me was another attempt at a cash grab, with this co-lender attempting to hold the project hostage in the hopes of getting a bigger piece of the pie. Refusing to grant a third—a third!—renewal amounted to a shakedown that was both shameless and inappropriate.

In the face of more obfuscating and excuses, I finally had to tell the participating bank president that he was an incompetent asshole compounded by the fact that he was being a moron before our very eyes. I told him I didn't have time for his BS and that he needed to grow up.

This bank president didn't seem to like those comments, and he turned to the lead bank president.

"Are you going to let him talk to me like that?" he asked.

I don't know what he was hoping for, but the lead bank president didn't even respond to him. He probably agreed internally, because this other bank president was causing him a lot of problems. No one was in any doubt about what was happening or why, and I expected the lead bank president to turn around and come down on him, setting him straight and getting the project back on course.

That didn't happen either, and the spineless display in front of me was almost as sickening as their asshole behavior. Nothing was getting resolved, and I saw crystal clear what was happening to this project that I'd put together and its subsequent success.

This meeting was only going to end one way, my way.

"Screw both of you!" I said, telling them the project was all theirs.

I walked out the door. It was a sore thing to have to lose this project and the future earnings from profit, but working with these guys was no longer an option and would cost me something much more, my sense of dignity. There was no possible way I'd roll over for them and continue working for them to take all my hard-earned profits. If they wanted to rip this development out from under me, the least they could do was figure out how to carry it forward on their own.

Considering what I'd seen so far in my life from banks that pulled loans and took possession of real estate projects, it never worked out all that well for them.

A swift exit from this development ended up having a serious silver lining to it, and the timing of this whole thing ended up being perfect for me and just as horrible for the banks. A year later, the great real estate market we'd been enjoying had dried up, and conditions in residential development were taking a serious nosedive.

If I'd been able to stick with the project, I'm sure we could've toughed out another year of strong sales, putting us in line with our modest projections, but the time-consuming disruption the banks created ended up leaving them with a situation where new home sales went south. Timing is everything!

Their attempt to get more out of the deal was going to leave them with much less.

All that remained then were the details of the note, which was originally for $1,500,000 in development and construction expenses. Payments were either based on a monthly minimum or the net proceeds of lot sales. The note was with the primary bank, and they had the other bank participating at 50%, something I'll say again that we weren't asked about nor gave our approval for.

The sales we did execute ended up paying the bank roughly $750,000, cutting the bank note in half and consisting of an average of three to four sales a month. The end result of the dispute between the banks and their un-renewed note was that we had no working capital and no funds whatsoever after all of the profit on sales went directly to the bank.

This process took place just before the time that the Resolution Trust stepped in and froze loans throughout NH, leading to so many of the other headaches I've already described in previous chapters. Here I managed to dodge a bullet that would've been coming anyway, but I was already out of the project and able to walk away.

The banks took over and were in possession of the development project, but they had some buyer's remorse after discovering their suddenly poor prospects that made them decide to enter into a dispute with me.

Once again, the bank had made a terrible misstep that cost them dearly, because they knew I was personally insolvent on the project after already giving them everything, and coming after me for more was a useless, unproductive, and quickly resolved endeavor. Now they had the remaining lots and construction expenses on their balance sheets, not to mention builders that turned lukewarm about continuing with the development considering the banks status.

Bottom line: each brother owned their dairy farms mortgage free. The exchange farmer received the value of his farm, and the banks lost $261,000 each!

This action did not affect the brothers or the farmer involved in the exchange as they were no longer a party to this transaction.

The story is a great example of a financial institution's incompetent meddling in a functioning successful operation, snatching defeat from the jaws of victory in a way that cost them dearly. The real estate new home market remained strong for the next year. Had the two bank presidents not been such assholes, the chances are that the loan would have been paid off completely.

This deal went off the rails because of a dispute between two bank presidents. When a deal with a bank goes off the rails, it almost never gets back on track. From everything I've seen, it all boils down to two things: greed and incompetence. These are people who want to be spending their lives working with money, yet their myopic focus on it prevents them from doing almost anything else. As soon as they start trying to make decisions on real estate, the markets, or contract terms, they end up shooting themselves in the foot.

I don't know what it is or why people working in these positions tend to behave this way, getting in over their heads when just servicing the loans would make them money. Maybe it's genetic or some kind of congenital defect, something in the water, who knows. It leaves me wondering, as I have so many times throughout the years, how these banks stay in business.

Mothers, don't let your children become bankers.

chapter ten

Jim Masiello and the New Hampshire State Board of Education

Although my business accomplishments are what I'm primarily known for now, it's worth shifting gears and looking back to when I was something of a political wunderkind. The political arena can be beautiful in its simplicity. An election happens, someone wins, and everybody else loses.

I was building a presence in the business and political realms that didn't stop once I left office as mayor of Keene. Perhaps the most impressive political feat I accomplished was the role I played helping to elect John H. Sununu to New Hampshire's governorship in 1983, which began a family dynasty in statewide office that included his two sons. The impact I had is still being felt, as Chris Sununu occupies the governor's office to this day.

When John was running, I used as much muscle as I could to get him into office. That included campaigning around the state and Keene region, writing messages, attending fundraisers, and talking him up everywhere I could. It may have made the difference, because John defeated liberal incumbent Hugh Gallen by only around 13,000 votes.

After he was sworn in, I told the governor that if he ever needed me to help in his administration, I would try to work it into my schedule. My only condition was that I couldn't walk away from business and family responsibilities. He probably heard offers like that, and there were droves of people clamoring for administration positions, so I didn't think much of it. But not many people had put themselves out there for him to the extent that I had.

It wasn't long after that I got a call from him telling me that he needed my help. Getting a call from the governor was always nice, and I told him I'd be happy to hear him out.

Of all the things he could've dropped in my lap, what he came to me with was an issue with the state board of education. He was quickly discovering that they were an ineffective body, sclerotic, and that they were ignoring or oblivious to many advances in educational technology and pedagogy that students and teachers in the state needed.

I asked about the makeup of the board, and it turned out that the previous governor had appointed all of them. Gallen was a Democrat who had selected social service workers or those with other state positions to the board, leaving it glaringly lacking anyone with a business background.

What we had to do was modernize the New Hampshire State Department of Education, and we started tossing around ideas for how we could get that done. Since I'd been on the Keene Board of Education, I had a good grasp on the dynamics of what was in play and how the educational bureaucracy functioned, even if this was at a larger scale. We were able to identify the needs of the department and what it would take to get it there, and all John needed was someone to spearhead the effort.

But my experience also taught me how resistant some can be to change in a department of education, and I had some expectations for the governor as well. If I was going to step into a role here, he needed to support me in any decisions that I made, and that included terminating the entire board and replacing them with successful business types. That wasn't going to be an issue for him.

I received a unanimous confirmation vote from the governor's counsel and was confirmed as chairman immediately after the vote by the governor taking on a position at a time where there was a lot of work to do and a lot of pressure to make progress on it. This was a big responsibility, but I felt I was up to the task. One significant detail of how the board operated was that they only met in Concord, the capital city, which I didn't think was effective because the members weren't familiar with what was going on around the state.

Immediately shaking things up, I had the board convene about forty miles away in the high school of another town and invited members of the community. We had a one-hour open hearing session, where any attendee could express concerns or ask questions. Considering the board had never traveled out of Concord and the people here had never had this kind of opportunity, I had a feeling the other board members might end up feeling a tad nervous.

Because of my notoriety as the controversial mayor of the third largest city in the state, the media seemed to take a lot of interest in all of this, adding to the pressure and the level of scrutiny, but there were also some benefits to having the press involved as well.

I knew one of the reporters quite well, and he told me that the board was going to try to get me to resign at that meeting. While I was a conservative businessperson and they weren't, what they were really angry about was that they had to leave the capital and drive to get to the meeting.

As the commissioner and I rode to the meeting, he urged me to stop at the state gas pumps to fill up for the eighty-mile round trip. Aghast, I responded that I could afford gas and that it didn't need to be an expense for the state taxpayers. He shot back that all the other board members would be doing it. I put an end to that practice immediately, giving these board members yet another reason to be angry. Several of them had been refused gas by the state then and there.

I convened the meeting, recognized members of the board, and explained the rules to the board members. The plan was to start with an executive session, which meant only board members could be in attendance, so it was only us there for the time being.

The board had a woman who might be best described as the ringleader of the group, and I asked her if there was anything she wanted to say. She said that she did. I asked if it was a personnel issue, and she confirmed that it was. The next step was to say that I as chairman would go into the executive session for the purpose of a personnel issue, and when I did that the other board members looked at me quizzically.

They were sensing that in this small instance I was deferring to the interests of this woman, and when we got into the executive session, I told the board members that I knew most of them and was familiar with their histories and experiences. I explained how no one had any doubt that we wouldn't get along very well, but because I was the chairman after a unanimous vote by the governor's counsel, they were stuck with me, and things would be done my way.

I could see on their lips that they wanted to try to find a way to get rid of me already, but the picture I painted was that it was not going to happen. I turned the tables, telling them that the only way out of this situation was if they resigned, and I strongly suggested that they should. And if they didn't, it was not going to be pleasant for them if they wanted to stick around just to attempt to roadblock what needed to get done. You could've heard a pin drop.

I wasn't mean about it, just firm, and after the meeting I met with each and every board member to individually explain the situation and come to a resolution. All but two who did have some experience ended up accepting the situation and resigned from the board, leaving me plenty of seats to fill with people who could help me bring the department of education into the present.

As promised and planned, I then went about recruiting those with business backgrounds to the state board, but don't think for a second my only criteria was anyone who'd been able to make a few bucks. Each had local school board experience as well in addition to a passion for education and a drive to make a contribution that would improve the lives of our students.

The task before us was clear: automate and modernize the department of education's systems. At the time, the entire department only had one Selectrix typewriter, a stunning fact that meant the whole operation was running more or less in the Stone Age. We had to computerize the department, and to help with this we consolidated the department's three offices.

At my request, the governor set up a meeting with the head of the state's IT department, but he was another previous democrat appointee who loved gold jewelry and was not likely to be cooperative. Why anyone would stand in the way of these attempts to modernize was beyond me, regardless of their backgrounds or affiliations. Education doesn't stand still, and there's always a way to improve. Way too many people wanted to consider the job done and the mission complete as they floated through.

We met in the governor's office, and the head of IT walked in wearing an open-collared shirt, gold chain around his neck, and gold on his wrist. The look was both unprofessional and gaudy, and the meeting did not get off to a good start.

I asked him why the Department of Education hadn't been automated and that bringing in the necessary technology wasn't even on his schedule.

He said he'd get around to it sometime. Oh boy.

"You do know that this department is the largest in the state, with seven thousand teachers, none of whom know what's going on around them, right? Their continuing education credits are written on 3x5 index cards, for crying out loud. Automating the service of education is the single most important task in front of us."

He looked at me. I looked at him. His gold neckless was kind of dangling there. The lack of cooperation was galling, and it registered with me that this was not going to work. Not only was he not going to help, but I could see how easily he could make things worse. I didn't think he was fit for his position like most Democrats appointed by Gallen and didn't want him getting in the way.

So, I did what was necessary and told him that I'd get it automated myself and that I didn't want him getting involved, not that he was about to anyway, and causing more problems. I told him to get the Hell out of my way. I asked if we had an understanding, but all I got back was a semi-stunned look before I got up and walked out of the meeting. I had work to do and couldn't be wasting any more time with him or people like him.

Part of the challenge of modernizing everything was getting an accurate accounting of what was going on, and to do that as I mentioned we needed to get everything into a single place. Three different offices resulted in way too many employees with a lot of redundancy, overlap, and general waste.

I took the leases for the department's three offices to my oceanfront home and read them with a six pack of beer. Documents like these were already very familiar to me from all the work I'd been doing, and I quickly zeroed in on the termination clauses to see what they said. It turned out the state was paying two groups of my Republican friends a half million dollars a year to occupy space in their buildings, and this was when there was no termination penalty, making it very attractive to get up and leave.

The challenge though was finding a place to go, and I started looking around for one state-owned building where we could house the entire operation. Luckily at that time the state had just vacated a building that had been used for mental health purposes, so I had the governor arrange a tour of the building for us.

Along with the governor, the commissioner, and a couple of others, we went to check out this building to see if this was space that would accommodate our needs. The building had previously been housing people with severe mental disabilities in small rooms that would make great offices now that they were empty, and there were larger rooms for cafeterias, meetings, conferences, and other functions.

It seemed perfect, at least to me after I had to warn the commissioner that if he wanted to keep his job, he had better not pull the usual political BS of introducing any politics into this process, which he was known for doing with the Democrats under Governor Gallen. I also warned him privately when I took over that he gets one chance and if I catch him playing political games, he would be gone in a flash. So, we went ahead and notified the current building landlords that we'd be terminating the leases and then went about the process of moving everything into the new building. Within ninety days, we were all squared away with a new building and a new direction for the department that would lead to a higher degree of organization and efficiency. A number of positions that weren't necessary any longer were terminated. The department had numerous "consultants," and at my request we terminated all of them.

Our next task after the move was to work with the staffing and accounts aspects of the department to see how that could best be automated. There were seven thousand teachers to support across sixty-three districts, and I put together a team of business CFOs from various industries around the state along with a superintendent of a very well-run district to look at how we could bring automation to the department.

We knew we had a challenge in front of us, but it wasn't all grueling work. We managed to even have a little fun in the process.

One day I got a call from the commissioner of education, and he said there was a building just up the hill from us that had a lot of mentally challenged patients. They found out about our occupancy and had evidently taken their new neighbors to heart, because according to him we had a whole bunch of commissioners of education now.

If the ripple effects of our move ended up inspiring those folks with challenging circumstances in some way, that seemed like icing on the cake.

We kept moving forward with our automation plans, and within six months we secured assistance from a New Hampshire computer manufacturing center, which would both get us where we needed to be and bolster high-skilled jobs in the state.

But it wasn't easy, and it became apparent to me that one of the biggest challenges we faced had to do with the New Hampshire Education Association, a part of the National Education Association. The teachers' union wasn't involved with the state board in the past, so I invited them to state board meetings and had the commissioner arrange a personal meeting. That gave me a chance to express that, while I wasn't a big fan of the union, I did want to work with them and give them room to participate in the state board meetings as long as they met certain conditions. The condition was that these board meetings weren't a place to air grievances about teacher compensation, benefits, days off, etc. They were all about improving students' education, and they could contribute to those discussions on those grounds.

I thought I was being fair, productive, and even relatively inclusive doing that, but the next thing I knew the commissioner was showing me some articles with one in particular alleging that the "state board chairman is against teachers," using quotes out of context and general misrepresentations.

I summoned the union head person to my office at the department and asked where they got some of these quotes. She said, "Well, that's what we observed."

It seemed like they needed some education, and I was about to give it to them.

"OK, here's what we're going to do the next time you put out a communication to 7,000 teachers with anything negative about me or the board, consisting of made-up statements that neither I nor the board said. I'm going to send a letter to every single one of your teachers telling them how ineffective your association is, and I will describe all of it. I can afford to do this and will the very next time this happens again. You'd better start participating in a positive way, or you will not be involved."

I wish that message had gotten through and that was the end of problems with the teacher' union, but it wasn't. While they didn't trash talk us to their members again, and I didn't need to send a letter out to every teacher in the state, it seemed like they were just biding their time to stir up more trouble.

With about a year to go, the board at my suggestion appointed a group of seventy-five people to assess how we could improve the quality of student education in all aspects. The union issued a minority report damning the actions while saying nothing about helping students. It was a flaming hot pile of garbage, and I wasn't going to let it pass by without a forceful response.

With press in attendance, I made a statement that the greatest threat to the quality of the education in this country was the National Education Association. It was a bold thing to say and actually got the attention of some national news outlets.

After butting heads with the old board members, the state's IT department, and the teachers' union, I still had to go through one last battle with the legislature before my time as chairman of the state board of education was up.

On one particular occasion, the state legislature was having a budget hearing on the Department of Education. Since there were no apparent issues, I elected not to attend. But while it was going on I got a call from the commissioner, telling me I needed to hurry up and get over there, because the chairwoman of the Legislative Finance Committee wasn't allowing any of the department officials to respond to the committee's questions.

One of the items in our budget was a $5 million request for enhancing educational technologies, something we'd all agreed in advance to support, but now she was trying to shoot it down.

The committee took a lunch break, and I headed to the capital at break-neck speed. I didn't run any red lights, but I hurried as fast as I could, and the chair had just reconvened the meeting when I walked in. The chairwoman lowered her eyes at me and offered this warm welcome.

"Well, here is our state board chairman. To what do we owe this honor?"

It was as good an invitation as any to get right into the issue, and I announced to her in front of the entire room and all those in attendance that she had been conducting a disrespectful hearing. Everyone around became silent as the confrontation deepened.

I said, "For your edification, this is a hearing, and you should be listening, but instead you've chosen to pontificate your uninformed views."

Our discussion at the hearing didn't get us very far, and with our technology budget on the line, the speaker of the house interrupted the process and asked that we head to the governor's office. We did, the speaker, chairman, commissioner, and me. It was still unpleasant, but at least behind closed doors in the presence of the governor I was able to speak a little more freely. "Screw you!" I told her, and in truth she deserved something much harsher than that. We had discussed the hearing prior, and she had said it would be an automatic passing of the budget. What really pissed me off was that she was from the "north country" (northern NH) and was a fellow Republican and, up to that point, a friend.

It was quite an experience serving as the chairman of the New Hampshire State Board of Education. Old board members needed to be pushed out, others needed to be told off, some needed to be stepped over to get things done, but my guiding star was always improving outcomes for students, and those ends justified just about any means.

I vividly recall my first meeting with all principals and superintendents of the sixty-three districts. When I was introduced, three of my former teachers and coaches were looking a little stunned. No doubt it seemed off to them that with my past reputation I could be the head of NH schools. Boy, I could have told some interesting stories which would lead to wonder how in hell I ever got to this point.

We had a lot of accomplishments. We introduced the first "gifted and talented academy" student program into all of New Hampshire's sixty-three school districts, made a course in personal finance a high school graduation requirement, and consolidated and automated the entire department.

Interestingly, my first assignment as chairman resulted from a call from the governor asking me to accompany his wife Nancy to a meeting of Fortune 100 executives at the DC home of VP Bush. Within a week I was at the meeting when the VP spotted me and came to say hello. His first words were, "Jimmy, what are you doing here?" He had not been told that I was the new state board chairman, which was what the meeting was all about: gifted and talented student programs. We had a nice but brief visit. When we got back to NH, I immediately set up an academy where teachers would attend on weekends to understand how to identify and handle the very bright students.

For me at this point, it was back to the private sector, where I could happily leave the infighting and politicking to others. I'd done my job at the request of Governor Sununu to modernize the state's Department of Education, I was satisfied with what we'd accomplished, and I was ready to move on. If only everyone in government could say the same.

chapter eleven

Jim Masiello for New Hampshire

Although my political career is really just a fraction of what I've done in my life, it's an area I take a lot of pride and satisfaction in. Being a public servant is an honor, a privilege, and a great responsibility when others are entrusting you to further their welfare and improve their lives.

And when it comes to higher office or statewide offices, the gravity of that responsibility should give even the most ambitious among us plenty of pause.

There are those out there who feel like these roles are what they were born for, those who feel like they are called upon by others to stand up, and then there are those who come within reach of them just because of an unusual set of circumstances.

For me, I felt like all the doors opened easily when it came to politics. The New Hampshire Republican Party was where I belonged, and it fit like hand in glove with all the community and state projects I was involved in. With each successful campaign or project, it built a larger place for myself where more people knew me, my presence across the state increased, and my appetite for playing a role in public policy grew.

Despite the usual contentiousness and strife that can come from participating in local politics, I viewed my time as mayor of Keene as an unequivocal success and a launching pad for bigger and better things. Getting reelected with 70% of the vote will do that to you, and it gave me a lesson that my brand of politics and my ability to get things done were a winning combination.

When I announced my intention not to run for mayor again, it was the first of many difficult decisions. Although there are no end of advisers, aids, and campaign managers in politics, being the candidate means you have the final say about what you do, and there's no roadmap for exactly where your political career will take you.

Hindsight is 20/20, and a simple twist of fate can be all that separates the legends of our time from those who are quickly forgotten.

The natural progression for successful mayors is to consider a run for the governorship, and that was a position I seriously explored launching a campaign for based on the encouragement of several newspapers and other political operatives. But as with any statewide office, the stakes are much higher and the competition much steeper. Sure, I had an incredible success story and a record I was proud to run on, but all across the state others were having their own successes and eyeing their own promotions to Concord as well.

There was even a group that formed with the explicit goal of getting me to run for governor, certainly a welcome sign for any potential candidate that signaled an easy route for donations, volunteers, and campaign evangelists ready to carry my message.

But my personal calculations for what to do couldn't place too much credence on the calls from this group, and you know if I felt like I was right for the job I wouldn't let anybody else in the state deter me or intimidate me when it came to starting up a campaign of my own. I don't let anybody stand in the way when I'm fighting to get something I am very qualified to handle.

The overriding sense I had was that running for the governorship right after being mayor was not the right time. I was still very young, and I had deep concerns that everything I had done still wasn't enough to get me there. Building a stronger network of allies and developing a statewide platform was going to be necessary, and in a matter of years after doing that it was reasonable to think I could coast into the governor's chair.

The accomplishments of my time as mayor of Keene weren't going to fade away. I had time on my side to stack the deck in advance of my run. And the last thing I wanted to do was rush into it prematurely and take a loss, because when people all across the state invest so much time and energy into you only for it come to nothing, it's easy for your support to fizzle out and your star to dim.

Some polls that came out painted a mixed message about this decision to wait on a campaign for the governorship. It was fascinating to see on a map how strong my support and visibility were in southern and western New Hampshire. Even southern New Hampshire from the seacoast west appeared to be solidly in my corner.

As anyone even slightly familiar with the granite state knows, these are some of most heavily populated regions in the state, and to see how much support I had from them was a colossal boost, making the path I was on crystal clear.

Keep at it. Maintain visibility. Create inroads with more northerly parts of the state. Pick the right moment to run.

That was my plan, and I threw myself at it with gusto, becoming incredibly active and influential with local and statewide government organizations, political groups, and connecting with current office holders. Every day was an opportunity to make a new connection and take another step forward when it came to building the support I needed.

But not everything was going according to plan, and that included some demographic shifts that made New Hampshire a very evenly divided place, politically speaking. While many in key roles were Republican activists, and New Hampshire as a whole had a well-deserved reputation as a fiscally conservative state, an influx of people moving in tilted its leanings.

An exodus from Massachusetts had a dramatic impact. When people got sick of the taxes there, they'd end up migrating north, and in the process all those people would pull New Hampshire more in the direction of Massachusetts. Much the same can be said of Vermont, which used to be ruby red until newcomers overwhelmed the resident population and tilted voting results to the far opposite end of the political spectrum.

This wave of migration didn't mean fiscal conservatives couldn't get elected in New Hampshire, but it did mean they had to be smart, diligent campaigners, and they couldn't take anything for granted. I had a front-row seat to how these new dynamics were playing out, and I was committed to learning everything I could while playing the biggest role I could.

As of course happens, time passes, and the next round of elections began to loom large on the horizon. Those of us on the fiscally conservative side began looking for ripe targets when it came to unseating unsavory incumbents, and speculation started up about who would step up to challenge them from our camp.

The goal for me was to come out early and back an eventual nominee who would then remember my critical support and return the favor once they got elected and made it into office. This kind of behind-the-scenes jockeying happens in advance of every election in what's now referred to as a "shadow primary," and I was committed to advancing someone I could both genuinely support and felt could in turn help me.

The biggest target in this particular year was a senator by the name of Tom McIntyre, who was someone we all felt needed to go at the very first possible moment and relished the thought of playing a role in his banishment from the office. For those of us in favor of fiscally responsible governance, we found him to be an embarrassment. His views were diametrically opposed to ours, and sometimes it felt like he didn't even belong in the state.

That impression fed on his glaring lack of presence in the state. "Where's Tom?" became the common refrain, and there was plenty of evidence that he'd more or less abandoned the state that he was representing. It seemed like after two terms in office he became very acclimated to living in Washington D.C. He bought a condo there while maintaining a single room apartment in Dover, New Hampshire, though he seemed to only set foot there once in a blue moon.

We were all convinced that Tom had fully crossed over into being a D.C. resident in all but name only. The lifestyle of the rich and famous, glitz and glamour, had gone to his head, and that's as far away from the hard-working, mostly rural lifestyle in New Hampshire as you could get.

It was time to roll up our sleeves and get this guy out of office, but first we needed someone to run against him. I know what you're thinking, and the answer is no. I didn't immediately put myself out there and declare my candidacy. I had my plan and was sticking to it, with the United States Senate seeming much less appealing because of the constant travel and the huge amount of time away from home.

We instead coalesced around a highly qualified Manchester attorney named Warren Rudman to run against McIntyre, and I was excited about the prospect of getting on board with him early and pulling out all the stops to get him into office. This was in concert with the Republican National Senatorial Committee and our statewide Republican committee, all of whom were fully on board with this choice. The ducks were getting in a row, and we were beginning to plot out our campaign strategy.

I was getting myself in great position as well. They asked me to be chairman of the committee to elect Warren, and let's just say they didn't have to ask twice. This was going to be a great position for me where I could maintain my visibility and influence the campaign, all while furthering my career and advancing my policy agenda.

As we began to ramp up our operations, getting into the early phases of decisions related to staffing, offices, and a calendar of events, I received a phone call one evening from Warren, who asked me to come out the next morning to Nashua for breakfast. He had something important on his mind that he wanted to talk about.

Now, I didn't know Warren all that well, but he was a close friend of a former governor Walter Peterson, who I did know well and admired, and a mysterious request like that immediately got my mind turning into knots. I wasn't an expert on everything Warren had done in his life. Was there a skeleton in his closet he was about to unleash on me that could doom the campaign? Did he have some weird or unusual policy position on some issue that I was going to have to swallow? Maybe it was something good and he had a role for me in mind in the future.

I met with him for breakfast the next morning torn between optimism and dread. Things started off nicely enough. He told me about his growing law practice and how he had two sons in college. As with his reputation, he seemed like a great guy with a good head on his shoulders. But then came the kicker. All those things going on in his life at the moment were compelling him to wait a bit longer until the next term before running.

He'd decided not to run for personal reasons, and that left me completely adrift. I found out first-hand what kind of problems arise when you back a horse too early. It may never even make it out of the gate.

There was no room for argument, no convincing him otherwise, and it was my job to turn around and deliver the news about what had happened to everybody else.

I rallied the troops and came out with the unpleasant news, which was disheartening to say the least. We'd already pinned our hopes on Warren, and now he was gone. Meanwhile, the fundamentals of the race were still the same. We agreed that the seat was easy to win, and all we needed was a viable candidate. We treated it like a foregone conclusion that Tom McIntyre would lose, and the only question was who would take his place.

With the beginnings of all the necessary campaign machinery set up and ready to run, the tracks were already laid for victory.

It didn't take long before the attention turned to me as a replacement candidate. Since Warren hadn't even announced his run, it wasn't like he was dropping out and I would be stepping up at the last minute, which would've been horrible. This was a chance to have my own campaign from start to finish with a fantastic group of enthusiastic people helping me run against an incumbent whose days were numbered.

No matter how nice and easy it sounds to slide into a senate seat, I quickly found myself weighing many of the considerations that Warren did. Being mayor or even governor of a small state is one thing, but stepping into the U.S. Senate is something else. It's inviting a national level of scrutiny beyond what most people could imagine and virtually no one could find comfortable.

And that was just the beginning of the demands. I'd already mentioned the travel, but then there's the need for fundraisers and other events that eat into your schedule. Even the job of a senator itself is a much different animal, with much of your success or failure dependent on ninety-nine other individuals from across the country.

Family strain is almost inevitable, and I wondered what it would mean for my family for me to be someone who was only around for the weekends most of the time. Still, I believed in myself and my ability to pull it off. It took several weeks of intense discussions with family and close friends, but I decided this was an obligation and my moment after all. I was ready to take my chance.

I launched my campaign for senate in early April.

Despite all the support and camaraderie I had when it came to my senate run, I was not the only one seeking the Republican nomination for the seat, which shouldn't be surprising. There's always intra-party competition, and it's the role of the primary to weed out everybody else.

In this year, there were a couple others in the party seeking the nomination. One was a commercial airline pilot who had been campaigning since the prior year. He was extremely conservative, which works out well in northern N.H., but seemed an unlikely choice because of his background. Another throwing his hat into the ring was the president of the New Hampshire State Senate, which was certainly more of a background that you would expect from someone seeking a seat in the U.S. Senate.

This guy really wanted the seat badly, but the problem with him though was that hardly anybody knew about him outside of Concord, the state capitol. Despite his position and his time in office, he had little respect or visibility anywhere, and it mostly seemed like the only thing he had going for him was a misguided sense that his current position entitled him to the statewide position.

It didn't work like that, but no one could tell him otherwise.

As I was finalizing my decision and thinking through my campaign game plan, I got a call from Jim Baker, an attorney, statesman, and politician who people might remember as a key player in the Reagan and George H.W. Bush administrations. He was the 10th White House Chief of Staff, the 67th United States Secretary of the Treasury, and also the 61st Secretary of State before returning as White House Chief of Staff for Bush.

Baker was someone I'd met on several prior occasions and had an incredible amount of respect for. Calls from him were rare but always welcome, and I had a feeling he'd caught wind of my situation.

The call was straight and to the point. Baker was a very close friend of George H.W. Bush, who had left it to Baker to convey his personal request that I enter the race against Senator McIntyre. I was blown away that I was being called upon to do this after ending up tiptoeing toward the race in this roundabout way.

What was more, Bush 41, without my knowledge, had gone ahead and authorized a poll for me to get some data on how the race was shaping up, and the results were eye opening. The survey showed that I had a large lead assuming the president of the NH Senate got out of the race after accepting his dismal percentages.

Getting off the call, it was hard not to feel like the election was already half in the bag. I could see myself getting that win and becoming a senator, and the only thing standing in my way was a few months' time.

When the results of the poll became public, not everyone was as thrilled about how it turned out, of course. The state senate president took particular exception that the poll had been done behind his back and that he wasn't automatically receiving the uncontested support of the Republican Party's leadership apparatus.

While he got to sit and stew, which I hoped would be the wakeup call for him that he needed to drop out of the race, I busily got to work launching my campaign and getting everything to full steam ahead. Congressman Jim Cleveland, whose campaign I was very involved with and who was a personal friend of the NH senate president, personally appealed to him to drop out of the race, but that only rankled him more.

Part of this involved meeting with other office holders in the party to curry favor for endorsements and other measures of support. The Republican National Senatorial Committee was in charge of doling out support for senatorial candidates, and they summoned me to Washington D.C. to begin getting familiar with their team and aligning on plans and strategies for carrying out the campaign.

I arrived and was set to meet with Congressman Cleveland and Senator Bob Packwood, who was without a doubt very arrogant. The congressman was there waiting for me in the senator's anteroom, and we spent the next thirty minutes waiting for the senator to make himself available for our scheduled appointment.

The clock ticked, we waited, and after more than thirty minutes I had to tell the congressman that I was at risk of being late for my flight and that I had to go. He understood, and nobody could explain the senator's strange absence from our meeting. We got up and were just about to exit through the door when Senator Packwood wandered in at the very last second without much apparent regard for being so late. We followed him into his impressive, historic office, the exact kind of space I hoped to create for myself when I came to town to take my position.

I didn't hesitate to tell him that we were running late thanks to his schedule, and he didn't beat around the bush or waste time with pleasantries.

"What makes you think you should be a U.S. Senator?" he asked, looking me in the eye.

"Well, Senator, just sitting here waiting for you and observing your arrogant attitude and disrespect for my schedule, I feel highly confident that I would make an exceptional senator."

While a lesser man might've been offended by that, it only took that many words for me to show him that I was on his level and had the fortitude to look out for myself.

The meeting wasn't much longer than that, but something clicked. I always felt sure the Bush endorsement factor is what made things happen for me. Shortly afterward, the RNCC made a significant campaign contribution to me and even assigned election staff to work the campaign and collaborate with my campaign management team. It felt like another door was opening, and the mere momentum of everything that was happening was going to carry me through it.

We launched the campaign in earnest with official statements, big kickoff events, and great fanfare. It was wondrous to behold for me to see everything humming as we got into the action. I had an excellent and heavily experienced staff and very dedicated supporters, all of whom looked up to me. We crafted a great message that aligned with my views and built upon my record as mayor and other accomplishments.

And best of all, I had fun doing it and felt like I wanted the job. Seeing the smiling faces, shaking hands, and hearing stories from people, it all motivated me to work hard to win so that I could keep working hard and make a difference for all of them in a new role.

We'd spend three or four days a week traveling around the state, getting as many miles under our belts as we could while away from our new campaign headquarters in Concord. From Portsmouth to Nashua to Manchester, we'd then go upstate to Laconia, Conway, Littleton, and Berlin. And so many more cities and towns in between. It was a blur but an unforgettable one. Win, lose, or draw, what a special experience it was meeting so many wonderful people.

Meanwhile I had a wife and three young kids at home, though they sometimes accompanied me at campaign events, and I had a young but profitable business that I ran concurrently and still had to devote some of my attention to. There was never a moment's rest, and this went on for four months.

Many might've found this schedule grueling, but these kinds of packed days were what I've known my entire life. I was ready to outwork anyone, staying true to myself and running a campaign I could be proud of with tons of great people.

Thinking back to that period, I still remember spending hours with my driver on small back roads and little towns way out of the way. I wanted every single vote I could possibly get, and there were no lengths I wouldn't go to reach that next one. Out on the road, we saw a beautiful side of New Hampshire that even lifelong residents rarely get to see. It's a wondrous place with so much to offer.

In addition to the events, the crowds, and the speeches, yes, there were also the always important fundraisers to help us keep the coffers full. Maintaining all this campaign machinery was not cheap, but I was bringing in enough and seemed to be striking the right balance between voter outreach and fundraising.

Time passed and the campaign chugged along. Our strong base of support remained rock solid. The polls continued to list me as the number one pick, but it was closer than I would've liked and certainly needlessly close. The stubborn state senate president continued to drag along with a modicum of support that any rational person would take as a sign that victory was out of reach.

To give you an idea of what life was like for me at this time, let me tell you about a typical day for us. I'd start the day at around 6 a.m. with a short morning run—have to make time for exercise, plus it gave me time to think. After racing through a shower, getting dressed, and breakfast, it was off for the first event of the day. Most often that was at the employee gate to introduce myself and ask for their vote.

From there we'd follow our schedule, which was largely determined by our campaign scheduler, as he handled requests from various support organizations scattered around the state. Lunch meetings. An afternoon or dinner event that was more public oriented. We'd have an internal meeting or call to discuss our progress and our plans. Sometimes that would mean dinner together, or there would be a fundraising dinner where I'd need to speak.

And then after that it was time on the road in the evenings getting to our next destination, possibly including a late check-in at a hotel depending on our destination. This was the way I lived, just nonstop on the go trying to meet with as many people as we could to get our message out at a breakneck pace.

Sometimes I miss that kind of life, but then I remember what happened.

Primary Day in New Hampshire was right around the corner, and we were greeted with another poll that didn't differ too much from the others. We had an edge on the pilot, Gordon J. Humphrey, with the state senate president siphoning off a percentage of our support. He had to drop out of the race for it to be a slam dunk win for me, but at this late stage of the game it was clear that he wasn't going to do that.

Since we were spending absolutely everything that came in for campaign contributions, our campaign finance committee put together a statewide fundraising effort to help us get over the finish line. That helped with our last-minute ad buys over the weekend preceding the election, ultimately allowing us to the numbers we thought we needed.

This all made the run-up to primary day a nail biter. Don't forget that I won my first term as mayor in a close contest, so I was no stranger to eking out a win, but this felt different. I was expected to win, and I expected myself to win. And yet it was apparent that it wouldn't be easy for reasons that none of us could readily understand.

Somehow my most prominent opponent in this contest was someone who'd never held elected office before and merely volunteered as an activist. He started off as a liberal. He was born in Connecticut, not New Hampshire. This guy should've been a footnote in the polls, not someone who was making it tight and on the verge of running neck and neck with me.

Something wasn't adding up.

Primary day came, and like a good citizen I cast my ballot. For a candidate, Election Day can be a strange affair. You've done everything you can do, and showing up at polling places begging candidates for votes at the last second can come off as desperate and unbecoming of a frontrunner. The only thing to do was try to sit back, relax, and hope that it would all work out as planned.

It didn't, as became clear that night. When all was said and done, I'd lost the primary race to Humphrey by a measly three thousand votes. The senate president came in dead last, garnering a pathetic total of thirteen thousand votes, many of which would have been mine. Victory had been snatched away from me, and in the aftermath of the election we finally figured out why.

It turned out that Humphrey had a wealthy significant other—they weren't even married until shortly after the primary election—and she had personally funded his long eighteen-month campaign, pouring in an unheard-of sum of money that had allowed him to overwhelm the race. We'd all seen the ads, but none of us knew the extent of them or what kind of impact they would have.

The pilot had managed to buy the primary race, which managed to take the prize over all our legwork, hustle, and show of force. Although it was a crushing defeat on one hand, on the other it was a hell of an effort, and I can't say I would've done much differently. Sometimes that's just the way the chips fall, missing out because of a guy with a bucketful of free cash and a Stooge who doesn't know when to quit.

And what happened next? Humphrey was able to cruise to victory in the general election, defeating Tom McIntyre by a comfortable margin in the same way that we all expected I would've done. Humphrey ended up serving two terms in the U.S. Senate before giving up the seat. He later tried to run for governor only to lose to the Democratic candidate. I have to think I would've done it better.

In my memory though, I remember much more than just the result of the race. When you encounter that many people, things are bound to happen, and even brief exchanges can take on a lot of meaning.

There was one older lady who followed me everywhere during the campaign. She was a pro-lifer who would show up to most of our events with her mentally challenged son. It got our attention when we found out she was writing "kills babies" with a felt-tip marker and writing them on cards that she would hand out to anyone who would take one.

One night as we were leaving an event, she interrupted me to give me one of the cards. We stared at each other for a long moment. There must have been at least twenty people standing there with us in the parking lot. I looked at her and thanked her profusely for being so kind and so generous by making this presentation.

We didn't see her or her mentally challenged kid again, and I was glad to have gotten through to her that I was someone worthy of her support, but for all I know she may have single-handedly thrown the election considering how close it was and how many cards she must've gone through.

My campaign for U.S. Senate was a great experience and one that I absolutely would repeat if I had it all back to do over again. Even though I was not victorious, I still valued making all those important contacts and gaining that kind of visibility.

In addition to the relationship I ended up enjoying with the Bush family, we also came in close contact with President and Mrs. Ford, who graciously stayed with us several times in our home. We attended a state dinner for the German Chancellor at the White House. And these family friendships ended up lasting for years and years, leading to cookouts with

George H.W. Bush and Barbara Bush. They'd stay with us while coming through New Hampshire on the campaign trail, which was a real treat for all of us.

There are lots of people who get to help candidates like them through donations or volunteering, but not everybody gets to put a roof over their heads for a night or share a laugh or a story with them in the morning before they head off to their next packed event. These are some of the memories and experiences that I've cherished the most in my time.

With this kind of reminiscence, my mind immediately goes to what might have been if things had been only a little different and I'd gotten those three thousand votes. Taking office, representing New Hampshire, and having my say on its behalf to influence important bills and the course of the country would have been a joy.

But how does that compare to what I ended up doing instead with SIAA in the insurance world? Certainly I didn't wait around for another election to run for something else, and my insurance work didn't stand still. Soon enough I was so locked into the course that I was on that going back to politics as a candidate never again seemed like the kind of prime opportunity it once did.

What I did do was revolutionize the insurance industry with an exciting new concept, touching millions of lives and having a profound effect on local economies in the process. I have to think that what I've done is at least equal in terms of tangible impact, even if it didn't come with the same level of fame a senate seat would. It paid much better though, and the sense of having a widely accepted entrepreneurial enabling model assisting and influencing the independent insurance distribution was greatly satisfying.

Being this close to that kind of a position taught me that the people who occupy these powerful positions are really just that, people. And they managed to get into their jobs by both the brute force of their own ambition and the lucky happenstance circumstances of how things turned out within our society.

There are all kinds of ways to influence the world around you—government, sports, charity, the arts—and I'm more than comfortable with a life spent building business achievements few others could dream of. Starting and running businesses are great ways to make a valuable contribution to our society, and I commend the people out there who are taking new business ideas and fighting to make them work.

In many ways what I went through was a precursor of what's become commonplace in elections and the government. Questions about the role of money, the merits of different experience, and what makes an ideal candidate are things we all collectively wrestle with. There are no easy answers, and these are things reasonable people can disagree about, but the most important thing is remembering our shared identity as Americans and all the common ideals and values that come with that.

Like with my business life afterward, I conducted myself as a politician in a way that was consistent with my beliefs, worked genuinely for the benefit of my constituents, and behaved in a way that my family and associates could continue to be proud of.

My life never had a specific roadmap to a particular destination that I had to get to, but whether it was the U.S. Senate or SIAA, it's clear that my focus, passion, and perseverance were going to get me to a successful outcome either way. I have always measured my business success by the strength of SIAA and our 5000 independent insurance agencies, who had the desire and work ethic to strive for greater achievements.

The message for people reading this should be that the same is possible for you even now, no matter what your current circumstances are. Take your failures and your defeats and turn them into monumental triumphs. Each step for me built on the last until I scaled high enough to get somewhere few had reached.

Remember, "success is a journey." My journey had taken me thirty-eight years to embrace and build on.

chapter twelve

Screw You—
And the Horse
You Rode in On

So, what are we supposed to make of all this? Compiling all these stories from detailed memories and writing them up like this leaves me with a few thoughts that stand out, but there's plenty of room for you to make your own interpretations. Mostly I hope reading about these situations, as faithfully described as I could, provided some entertainment for you. However, I did have a lot of chuckles playing with my adversaries' minds.

If you're feeling something along the lines of "better him than me," I understand that perfectly. But you probably also have some questions. Let me see if I can do a little mind reading and address some of the things you might be wondering about.

1. How could this really have happened to one person?

These stories do seem like a lot, especially reading them one after another, but they come far short of the full stories behind them. There were plenty of times where I could see these situations coming and had a feeling of "not again," but I suppose it was just my lot to have to deal with these things. I know some people who've never had to call a lawyer or meet a bank president in their lives, but in some ways these problems have been the price I've needed to pay for success.

One thing that did make a huge difference was the prudence involved in creating protected, irrevocable trusts for myself, my family, and my core businesses. Without that, I would've been far more legally exposed in some of these conflicts, which very easily would've turned out differently with me holding the bag.

That being said, it only takes being wiped out once to lose it all and never be able to come back from that. The luxuries I've enjoyed, the impact our financial comfort has had for my family, my business associates, these are things I can't take for granted after so many close brushes. Even though I'm retired, you might not be surprised to hear that I'm still doing some work, because just needing to have that impact and earn something for myself has been ingrained in my core from the very beginning.

Could I have stood for fewer problems along the way? Sure, but at the same time, considering how it all worked out, I wouldn't have done anything differently, even with all the headaches.

2. But stuff like this could never happen today, right?

Even though my days of wheeling and dealing in the real estate industry or building businesses are over for the most part, I still have quite a few friends and keep my ears out for a sense of what's going on. It might be easy to say, "Oh, that was the '80s and '90s—they had no idea how to do things back then," but back then we thought we were in the modern era at the height of sophistication.

So, yes, situations like these can and do still happen today. No amount of automation or technological innovation can completely eliminate things like human error, incompetence, and greed as long as people are still involved. The difference though is that the scale has changed. There are fewer community banks and less transparency with the large banks, so when they try to pull something on someone, there's an even greater chance that they'll get away with it.

3. What if you had to start all over again now or were just coming of age these days, could you be as successful?

I was tremendously fortunate with SIAA, but as I've tried to show, the root of all of this was a work ethic I was born with. In every age there are fortunes made and lost, opportunities that come and go, those who seize them and those who don't. I'd like to think that if I had to start over again, I'd be able to do just as well, but with speculations like that it's impossible to know for sure. I was able to juggle a lot of things in business at the same time until the RTC blundered their way into ruining many businesses. But after all my successfully wandering in various businesses for seven years got cut short by the RTC and banks' incompetence, I finally got back to SIAA as my only focus demanding my full attention.

My desk plaque stating, "**In the middle of every difficulty lies opportunity,**" is still my guiding light and can be a useful mantra for anyone. Yes, the world and our society have changed in the past thirty years, but one of the things I love most about America is as true as ever. Everyone has the freedom to turn over a new leaf and start something new, rising or falling on their own merits.

If you're reading this and feel a pang of jealousy about some of the things I've been involved in or the dollar amounts, here's what I'd say to you. What have you done to get yourself to the place you want to be? There are plenty of people who want more without doing anything for it. They want it all to be handed to them, but life doesn't work that way. Change scares the hell out of most people!

I can't guarantee anyone success, but I can guarantee this. If you get up off the couch and go after what you want, something will happen. Maybe you'll get rich. Maybe you'll just have a richer life for having made the attempt. Both are completely worthwhile results when compared to the alternative. Count on yourself, find the motivation, and continue to persevere even when things get tough. Luck is important, but I found that the harder I worked the greater the luck that found me.

4. Jim, my take on all of this is that you were just lucky. I mean, how stupid could those bankers be?

I personally wouldn't conflate luck with benefitting from mistakes that those at the bank made, even when they brought all the records of our leasing debt to the dump. I've had moments of good luck and have admitted as much, but what I've also done is put myself in situations where I was more likely to catch a break.

Given the way my estate and core business assets were protected, in reality I did not have to even respond to the banks' incompetence and demands. That would have been too easy. Instead, being very competitive by all standards, I chose the negotiation game and challenge with each and paid on the average of about forty cents on the dollar. Of that 40%, almost none of it came out of my pocket! As a matter of fact, I voluntarily paid $261,000 to a local bank that they did not know I owed from twenty-plus years ago. Hello!

Mostly, banks couldn't get anything from me that wasn't aggressively negotiated completely by me with my terms. They had to work for it all, and that created opportunities for them to make mistakes or accept my position. If I had simply gone along with them and their positions, I would've lost every time. That's because their interpretation of the circumstances was just biased in their favor; it wasn't because it was true and they were telling the truth.

With the IRS, I do think that deep down the statute wasn't updated intentionally, letting me off the hook when it came to the balloon I owed. Again, this came down to vigorously advocating for my position, so much so that even people at the IRS who were unable to accept it found themselves swayed by my conviction, possibly leading to actions that benefitted me, consciously or not.

5. Thanks for the book. What took you so long to get around to writing it?

People who know me have been telling me to write a book about these things for thirty years, especially my CPA John Burk and lead attorney Steven Burke, Esq. who graciously lived through war stories with the banks and the IRS. Usually someone would bring up the idea after a particularly inflammatory meeting where I had to point fingers and tell someone off. It took a long time for me to recognize that being faced with that kind of opposition, often incompetent and belligerent, was a notable thing.

I also hope to get the message across that it's OK to stand up for yourself and put people in their places if you are properly leveraged and your assets are secure no matter what kind of a disadvantaged position you might be in. There are those out there who would love nothing more than to act like they are better than you—whether it be because of where they live, what they've done, or who they are—and you are under no obligation to treat them with any deference because of it.

On the flip side, real respect comes from the kind of teamwork and collaboration we've had with my senior team at SIAA and with strategic partner insurance companies. My lead attorney since 1990 and my CPA who has been with me for over forty years have always been my sounding board as I never had time or patience for a board of directors. If you can work together with someone and try to build something important, you can respect each other and form a lasting bond. We've had plenty of mistakes and disagreements along the way, but when I know somebody's heart is in the right place, there's never any need for the kind of telling off many in this book have received.

6. Did you really say, "Screw you?"

I sure did, with enthusiasm! OK, that might be a PG euphemism in a few cases, but I can assure you that I freely said that and worse to idiots who demonstrated their ignorance compounded by their immense incompetence. I am not known for my patience, and rightfully so! So "screw you" is mild, especially for the bankers and their attorneys. It gets the tone and content across.

I have tried to leave out names as much as possible, focusing on positions instead, but some people who know me closely may be able to recall who some of these people were. As for everyone else reading, it's not the names that are important; it's the role they played and the responsibilities they had that were often flouted in an attempt to bring pressure on me.

Although I don't have many regrets in my life, mostly I regret the very few times when I should've said "screw you" but didn't out of a misplaced sense of amicability. People deserve to know when they're doing something wrong, and it doesn't have to be sugarcoated.

As we reach the very end, I'd like to reserve my final words for Kathy, my wife, as well as my three children and friends who've been with me along the way on this journey. They are the reason I kept getting up in the morning to fight these battles, that plus the adrenaline flowing to negotiate with what seemed like an army of incompetent bankers.

And the challenges of founding and growing the largest national Independent Insurance Agency distribution system, enabling and benefiting thousands of entrepreneurially successful agencies and their families made all the effort well worthwhile.

Family and friends are what's important in life, perhaps the only things that are truly important. It's easy to lose sight of that, but my impression with them leaves a more substantial legacy than any of the buildings or businesses I've built. All I could do was be myself along the way, and I send my love and appreciation for those close to me who've had to put up with it.

About the Author

JAMES A MASIELLO

Jim is the Former Founder, Chairman, and CEO of Alliance Holdings, Inc., parent company of Satellite Agency Network (SAN Group) and (Strategic Insurance Agency Alliance SIAA), a national network of over 5000 Independent Insurance Agencies writing over $10 Billion of premium.

Jim is also the founder of several successful Masiello Group entities including Financial Services, Insurance, Real Estate, Commercial Leasing, Real Estate Development, Employment Agency, and an American Express Corporate Travel Agency.

- **1983** - Jim created the Satellite Agency Network (SAN) Model. He wanted to grow his agency, and this model precluded investment in producers, branch offices, and agency acquisitions.
- **1994** - SAN had grown to 67 Independent Insurance Agency members in New England and New York State and was producing over $550 million in premium.
- **1994 & 1995** - The replication of the very successful SAN Alliance took place with the creation of the Strategic Insurance Agency Alliance (SIAA) with encouragement of National and Super Regional Companies and Consultants.

- **1997**—Under Jim's direction, SIAA began its national growth plan, utilizing well-known insurance consultants who formed the basis of the national Recruiting and Marketing program by partnering with identified Regional Insurance Agencies in each state, resulting in SIAA becoming the largest alliance of independent insurance agencies in the United States and a leading voice in today's insurance industry.
- At the end of 2020, SIAA had signed 49 Master Agency Partners, covering all 48 contiguous states with 5,000 signed independent insurance member agencies writing over $10 Billion in premium, making SIAA the largest independent insurance agency partnering national network.
- SIAA was recognized by Liberty Mutual and Travelers in 2019 as the only $1 Billion Independent Agency National relationships.
- Rough Notes Magazine has recognized SIAA as the number one largest Independent Insurance Agency Alliance for the past eight years.

In his tenure within the insurance industry:

- Considered an expert in the creative distribution of insurance services and products.
- Consulted and lectured on Independent Insurance Agency compensation and incentives for agency producers based on cross-selling initiatives.
- Received the Dr. Henry C. Martin Industry Achievement Award from Rough Notes of one of only six total recipients.
- Recipient of the Insurance Marketing and Management Services (IMMS) Marketer of the Year award.
- Served as President of the New Hampshire Life Underwriters Association (600+ agents).
- Chaired the New England Life Insurance Forum.

- Served on a number of insurance company advisory boards.
- Served on the Board of Heritage Insurance Holding Company.

2021 - Jim sold SIAA and subsidiaries in concert with Goldman Sachs following a one-year due diligence extensive process and founded:

- The Masiello Family Foundation—a multi-million-dollar Trust focused on assisting bright but financially challenged private school and college students on a scholarship basis.
- MFC Investco—a Private Investment entity.

Additionally:

- Served as the youngest Mayor of the City of Keene, NH for two terms.
- Recipient of "Citizen of the Year" award from the Greater Keene NH Chamber of Commerce.
- Chaired the New Hampshire State Board of Education for three years.
- Served as a Trustee for Southern New Hampshire University.
- Has been active in many insurance-related, community, political, and statewide organizations.
- Has authored numerous articles and has spoken extensively on insurance industry topics including agency marketing, agency valuations, cross-selling, and insurance distribution systems.

www.ingramcontent.com/pod-product-compliance
Lightning Source LLC
Chambersburg PA
CBHW031919240526
45464CB00021B/505